GRAY GOLDFISH

NAVIGATING THE GRAY AREAS TO SUCCESSFULLY LEAD EVERY GENERATION

STAN PHELPS

&

BRIAN DOYLE

Kate,
Thanks for
having me
out for the
Annual
conference.
Best,
Stan

PRAISE FOR GRAY GOLDFISH

"As a founder and CEO of multiple recruiting companies, I've seen how generational differences can make all the difference in recruiting and onboarding new employees. Brian & Stan's book is exactly what leaders today need to understand in order to Hire/Train/Retain the best talent possible and stay competitive!"

— BILL LAUGHLIN, FOUNDER, ORION INTERNATIONAL AND 11 OTHER COMPANIES, PRESIDENT, SYSTEMATIC BUSINESS CONSULTING

"With *Gray Goldfish*, Stan Phelps and Brian Doyle have written the ultimate playbook for every employer, human resource director, Fortune 500 CEO and small business owner on how to effectively engage and lead as many as five different generations in the workplace. From Matures to Gen Z, *Gray Goldfish* should be required reading for anyone who takes pride in transformational leadership."

— MARK BEAL, AUTHOR, *DECODING GEN Z: 101 LESSONS GENERATION Z WILL TEACH CORPORATE AMERICA, MARKETERS & MEDIA*

"Millennials are the largest generation in the workforce since the Baby Boomers, and Baby Boomers are working past the traditional retirement age. Meanwhile, Generation X is often lost in between these bigger groups. Learning to manage these existing and successive generations is crucial for organizational effectiveness and *Gray Goldfish* gives you the tools and insights you'll need to succeed."

— DAVID RENDALL, AUTHOR OF THE FREAK FACTOR, THE FOUR FACTORS OF EFFECTIVE LEADERSHIP, AND PINK GOLDFISH

"Brian Doyle and Stan Phelps have written a must-read primer for organizations committed to successfully leading a multi-generational workforce. Read this engaging book and learn from the best."

— CAROLYN A.M. BENYSHEK, DIRECTOR OF ADMISSIONS 2009-2017, UNITED STATES AIR FORCE ACADEMY

"Stan Phelps and Brian Doyle deal head-on with the new, unprecedented reality of bridging leadership across five generations in the workforce. Influenced by the vastly different socio-economic conditions they were raised in, they in-turn have vastly different needs and motivations. Leading solely from your own generational point-of-view can disenfranchise any of the other four generations now present, resulting in either turnover or groupthink. *Gray Goldfish* serves as a guide book to better understand what makes each generation tick; what motivates them, and what turns them off. Phelps and Doyle share real-world examples and practical cross-generational leadership tips that both corporations and governmental agencies have leveraged to their advantage. A great read on a workplace dynamic that can't be ignored."

— GEORGE SHERMAN, CHIEF EXECUTIVE OFFICER, VICTRA (VERIZON AUTHORIZED RETAILERS)

"*Gray Goldfish* offers an innovative and insightful approach to recruiting, managing and inspiring employees of all generations. The Generational Matrix it introduces is a compelling guide to personalized and authentic leadership that builds lasting employee loyalty."

— CHRIS MALONE, CO-AUTHOR OF *THE HUMAN BRAND: HOW WE RELATE TO PEOPLE, PRODUCTS & COMPANIES*

Spot on! One of the biggest concerns in the financial services industry is preparing for a massive inter-generational transfer of wealth from Baby Boomers/Gen X to Millennials/Gen Z. Brian's and Stan's research offers critical insight into the wants, needs, and attitudes of our future customers as well as providing a template for hiring and training the next generation of business leaders to meet this challenge.

— CHUCK EMBS, PRESIDENT/CEO, CHESME CAPITAL MANAGEMENT

Published by 9 INCH Marketing, LLC
Cary, North Carolina

Editing: Lee Heinrich
Layout: Evan Carroll

ISBN: 978-1-7326652-3-1
First Printing: 2019
Printed in the United States of America

Gray Goldfish is available for bulk orders, special promotions and premiums. For details call +1.919.360.4702 or e-mail: stan@purplegoldfish.com.

*This book is dedicated to my late brother John Phelps Jr.
A born leader, John had the ability to make everyone in the room feel
welcomed and valued. Whether you were 15 or 95,
he knew how to make you feel special.*

— Stan Phelps

*To my wife, Heidi, for always believing in me.
Her kindness will be felt by her family, friends,
and patients for generations to come..*

— Brian Doyle

CONTENTS

ACKNOWLEDGMENTS

Thank you to everyone who has inspired us, supported us, and/or shared examples with us for the book:

Shawn Achor, Lora Alexander, Jay Baer, Will Barfield, Mark Beal, Mike Beck, Josh Bersin, Connor Blakely, Ken Blanchard, Jeanne Bliss, David Bode, David Bowie, George Bradt, Madison Bregman, Deborah Brown, Mike Cannon-Brookes, Evan Carroll, Ron Carucci, Shravanti Chakraborty, Rosaria Cirillo Louwman, Steve Cody, Doug Conant, Vanessa Contreras, Tom Coyne, Cathy Davidson, Mary Lee Duff, Sherri Elliott, Theo Epstein, Emily Everett, Tom Feeney, Bob Filipczak, Melanie Frost, Marke "Hoot" Gibson, Jim Godwin, Scott Golas, Ian Golding, Bill Gore, Maddie Grant, Heidi Grant-Halvorsen, Shane Green, Steven Handmarker, Kevin Hazelwood, Brian Hart, Jeff Havens, Lee Heinrich, Lynn Herrick, Sylvia Ann Hewlett, Jim Holz, Shep Hyken, Carol Hymowitz, Matt Kalinowski, Rustin Keller, Beth Kwasny, Lynne Lancaster, Keith Langbo, John Mackey, Debra Magnuson, Angela Maiers, David Marquet, Melissa McLean, Lauren McGhee, Jacob Morgan, Vineet Nayar, Indra Nooyi, Jaime Notter, Chris Noyce, Larry Perlman, Claire Rainers, Hanna Rosin, Haydn Shaw, Simon Sinek, Emily Smith, David Stillman, Dave Swanson, Sarah Taffee, Art Taylor, Bruce Tulgan, Michelle Tunney, Brigitte Van Den Houte, Cindy Ventrice, Peter Ward, Robin Wells, Margaret Wheatley, Scott Wilson, Worth Wilson, Mike Wittenstein, Polly Young-Eisendrath, and Ron Zemke

FOREWORD

BY MARKE "HOOT" GIBSON

Leadership is about enabling every person on your team to contribute as much as possible to the success of the organization. At the same time, it's about helping them grow as individuals so both they and your team are better positioned for the future. Leaders, and I'm making a clear distinction between leaders and short-sighted managers, provide a vision that motivates and inspires their team to achieve more than they thought they could. At the same time, great leaders also supply the training and education individuals need to make your vision a reality. It's this balance of the strategic and tactical that makes seemingly disparate individuals into a highly-successful team. Striking the exact right chords with teams and individuals, however, is not an easy task.

If there's one thing I've learned leading thousands of people, in combat and peacetime, in the military and in civilian business, it's that there is no one-size-fits-all approach to leadership. Each individual is motivated by different things. Likewise, each person brings a unique perspective to problem solving and a unique skillset to the team. I see it on a daily basis in my role as President and CEO at NUAIR Alliance, a coalition of more than 200 private and public entities and academic institutions working together to operate and oversee Unmanned Aircraft System (UAS) testing headquartered in upstate New York. Some of my employees want every detail laid out for them before embarking on a project while others prefer high-level guidance and then want to discover the details on their own. Some prefer to work in groups while others prefer more independence. There are also those who prefer to drive hard for nine straight hours while others deliver results through more work/life integration. I even saw these differences as a two-star general in the Air Force. A common perception is that military personnel are all cut from the same cloth, but they too bring different approaches, styles, and perceptions to the fight. That also means they bring different leadership challenges.

I know from experience that generational differences play a role in how to best adapt your leadership style, but I never really had my arms around it until I read *Gray Goldfish*. By laying out why the generations are different and then how to use that knowledge, Brian Doyle and Stan Phelps have provided a leadership roadmap that every leader can employ immediately. Their Generational Matrix offers leaders a framework for how to approach successful leadership within the context of your own generation – identifying potential blind spots and ideal connection points. After reading the book, you'll be well versed on how to lead your team to achieve your goals while also developing better employees—of any generation.

I learned and laughed reading *Gray Goldfish* and I bet you will too. Enjoy!

– Marke "Hoot" Gibson, Major General, USAF, Retired
President & CEO
NUAIR Alliance, Inc.

INTRODUCTION

BY STAN PHELPS

"There is only one prediction about the future that I feel confident to make. During this period of random and unpredictable change, any organization that distances itself from its employees and refuses to cultivate meaningful relationships with them is destined to fail."

– Margaret Wheatley

In preparation for the 2018 season, the Phillies, Mets, Red Sox, Yankees, and Nationals all replaced veteran managers with younger skippers. The differences in age were marked. The five managers ranged from eight to 26 years younger than their predecessors. Some had no major league managing experience. According to Tom Verducci of *Sports Illustrated*, "the ability to connect with young players and a comfort with analytics rose above experience." These new managers were better at relating to the latest generation of players. One of them was 42-year-old Alex Cora who led the Boston Red Sox to a World Series title in his first year at the helm. This move by traditionally conservative baseball owners should be a wakeup call for today's leaders.

FIVE GENERATIONS

With the introduction of Generation Z (born starting in 1997) coming into the workplace, we now have an unprecedented five generations at work. Generation Z joins the largest group, Millennials, followed by Generation X, Baby Boomers, and Matures. It is not uncommon for today's leader to have team members that span 60 years from oldest to youngest. Speaking from experience, my father-in-law, Fred Wills, is 88 years old. He still works three days a week for the Town of Shelton, Connecticut.

The ability to relate and connect across these generations is vital. Each of the five generations brings their own unique expectations and needs. Sticking with our initial theme of baseball, Chicago Cubs manager Joe Madden believes that effective leadership and culture starts with relationships. Strong relationships lead to trust and trust leads to the willingness to exchange thoughts and ideas. That foundation breeds success.

For today's leader, the idea of managing teams that include five different generations is new territory. According to Carol Hymowitz in the *Wall Street Journal*, "That means they must create opportunities for young employees to advance (or risk losing them) while also making sure veterans, whose skills they need in today's tight labor market, don't feel overlooked. And to maintain productivity and innovation, they must persuade employees of disparate ages to collaborate."[1] They must effectively navigate the gray.

THE OCHO

Gray is the eighth color in the Goldfish Series. The original book, *Purple Goldfish*, focused exclusively on customers and how to add signature elements to their experience. It quickly became apparent to me that customers were only part of the equation. I learned that the companies who really got "it" for the customers, put an even greater emphasis on engaging their own employees. In the words of Ted Coiné in the foreword of *Green Goldfish 2.0 (co-authored with*

---

1. https://www.wsj.com/articles/the-tricky-task-of-managing-the-new-multigenerational-workplace-1534126021

Lauren McGhee), "You can't have happy enthused customers without happy engaged employees." Gold was the third color in the original trilogy inspired by lagniappe and the three colors of Mardi Gras. *Golden Goldfish* explored the ideas that all customers and employees are not created equal. The top 20 percent of customers drive 80 percent of profits. *Blue Goldfish* (co-authored with Evan Carroll) was next. It explored the impact of technology, data, and analytics on customer experience. The fifth color, *Red Goldfish* (co-authored with Graeme Newell), explored how being "for purpose" drives happiness and adds a sense of meaning for customers, employees, and society. *Pink Goldfish* (co-authored with David Rendall) returned to the marketing roots of Purple. It examined differentiation and how to create competitive separation in business. The seventh and last color before Gray was Yellow. *Yellow Goldfish* (co-authored with Rosaria Cirillo Louwman) looked at how companies can do a little extra to contribute to the happiness of its customers, employees, and society.

ENTER BRIAN

I met Brian Doyle back in 2013. I was engaged for a series of keynotes and workshops in Raleigh for Genworth Financial. The company is one of the main players in the mortgage insurance market. Brian was Genworth's VP of Marketing at the time and led a 20-person group responsible for strategy, marketing communications, public relations, customer experience, and customer/sales training. He supported a 75-person sales force and over 2,000 customers. We bonded over our collective interest in marketing and customer experience.

Over the next few years, I learned more about Brian's background. Originally from California, Brian went to college at the Air Force

Academy. Upon graduating with a degree in Physics, Brian became a commissioned officer and Air Force aviator. He served on active duty for nearly 10 years, mostly flying C-17s. The C-17 is the Air Force's primary strategic, large transport aircraft. At 174 feet in the length, it is a beast. Known affectionately in the Air Force as "The Moose," this nickname comes from the sound that is heard when the air is venting during refueling on the ground. It sounds like a moose bellowing. As the pilot and aircraft commander, Brian was in charge of the $225MM airplane and leading the crew. During his tenure, Brian led teams into combat situations as well as into austere and commercial locations in nearly every part of the world. Brian continues to be involved with the USAF, where he serves both as a Colonel in the Reserve and as an Admissions Liaison Officer for the Air Force Academy.

Through Brian's work in Corporate America and the United States Air Force, he's seen firsthand the challenges of managing across the generations. Brian and I are hoping to help you improve your relationships and drive engagement through our book *Gray Goldfish*. We believe the recipe for successfully leading across these five generations is not a one-size-fits-all solution. We believe the recipe comes from understanding nuances and being able to treat each team member as an individual. This involves going beyond the "Golden Rule" and treating others how you would like to be treated. *Gray Goldfish* implores you to treat others how they like to be treated.

Gray Goldfish is broken into four main sections:

Section I: Here we outline the "Why." The first part of the book explores the reasons for focusing on leading across the five generations and the origin of the Goldfish metaphor. We'll also provide an overview of each of the five generations and what makes them tick.

Section II: We uncover the "What" in this section. We'll share leading examples from the Gray Goldfish Project culled from over 75 case studies in eight major categories: Recruiting/Onboarding, Project Management, Recognition/Motivation, Flexing, Training/Development, Vision/Purpose, Feedback/Mentoring, and Retention/Loyalty. You'll see how other companies have instituted programs and policies to engage their employees effectively.

Section III: We'll share the "How" in Section III. In order to be an effective leader, we need to know how to lead every generation. Here we introduce the Generational Matrix, a handy reference tool. In addition, there is a chapter for each of the five generations. In order to lead every generation, you need to know how to lead *in the context* of your own generation. As a little extra, we'll also talk about the importance of followership.

Section IV: Closing it out, we share five final takeaways and offer suggestions for additional reading.

Ready to jump in and learn how to navigate the Gray? Let's go ...

PREFACE

"Friction and misunderstandings often occur when communicating across generations. It gets even more challenging when working across virtual settings."

– Raymond Arroyo

A DIVERSE WORKPLACE

Generation Z has reached the workplace. We now have to engage employees across five generations. Make no mistake, engaging today's workplace is vital to business success. Gallup reports that 85 percent of employees worldwide are not engaged or are actively disengaged at work.[2] There is a clear and recognizable need to equip today's leaders to ignite employee engagement across the generations.

Let's look at 10 compelling reasons to invest in leading across the generations:

10. DOLLARS AND SENSE

Firms that engage and enable their employees achieve up to 4.5 times more revenue growth than companies that don't.[3]

9. PEOPLE ARE PEOPLE

Employees need hope to be engaged. Gallup says that 69 percent of people who strongly agreed that their leaders made them feel enthusiastic and hopeful about the future were engaged. For those who strongly disagreed, only one percent of them were engaged at work.[4]

2. https://www.gallup.com/workplace/231668/dismal-employee-engagement-sign-global-mismanagement.aspx

3. https://www.kornferry.com/institute/employee-engagement

4. http://coaching.gallup.com/2015/10/the-four-things-followers-need-and-how.html

8. IT'S NOT JUST ABOUT YOUNG PEOPLE

71 percent of retirees who returned to work originally retired due to a lack of flexibility in their work arrangement.[5]

7. HORRIBLE BOSSES

75 percent of people voluntarily leaving jobs don't quit their jobs; they quit their bosses.[6]

6. ONE SIZE DOES NOT FIT ALL

87 percent of HR leaders consider improved retention a critical or high priority for the next five years yet 87 percent of employees are not engaged. As generational diversity increases, using a one-size-fits-all leadership approach is only making things worse.[7]

5. STUCK IN THE MIDDLE WITH YOU

We don't hear as much about them, but Generation X now holds 51 percent of leadership roles globally.[8]

4. SHOW ME THE MONEY

Companies who have highly engaged employees earn twice the net income of companies that don't.[9]

5. https://globalworkplaceanalytics.com/resources/costs-benefits

6. http://www.thesocialworkplace.com/2011/08/08/social-knows-employee-engagement-statistics-august-2011-edition/

7. https://www.kronos.com/about-us/newsroom/employee-burnout-crisis-study-reveals-big-workplace-challenge-2017

8. https://www.cnbc.com/2018/04/11/generation-x--not-millennials--is-changing-the-nature-of-work.html

9. https://www.ibm.com/talent-management/hr-solutions

3. RECOGNITION MATTERS

Forty-three percent of highly engaged employees receive feedback at least once a week compared to only 18 percent of employees with low engagement.[10]

2. MENTOR OR REPLACE

Should you mentor young professionals or just focus on having to recruit their replacements. 93 percent of young professionals say they left their employer the last time they assumed a new role. Taking care of current employees via effective mentoring is a lot easier and more cost-effective.[11]

… and the #1 reason for paying attention to how leaders manage across the generations:

1. SINCERITY AND TRUST

Of seventy-five possible drivers of engagement, the **ONE** that was rated as the most important was the extent to which employees believed that their senior management had a sincere interest in their well-being.[12]

10. https://temenosinc.com/resources/white-papers/employee-feedback/

11. https://www.gallup.com/workplace/236471/millennial-job-hoppers-seek.aspx

12. https://www.gallup.com/workplace/236483/enhances-benefits-employee-engagement.aspx

PART I

WHAT IS A GRAY GOLDFISH? (THE WHY)

CHAPTER 1

EVERYONE IS STRUGGLING WITH GENERATIONAL DIFFERENCES

"If you want to go fast, go alone.
If you want to go far, go together."

– African Proverb

As the business's President was wrapping up his latest story, I looked at the empty seat next to me. The meeting was supposed to have started five minutes ago and my analyst wasn't here yet. Then I heard it.

"Flip, flop, flip, flop, flip flop." I could tell by the frequency of the flipping and flopping that my 25-year-old analyst in her sandals knew she was late. She entered the room with a stack of papers to hand to the attendees and wearing a skirt that was a little shorter than I usually saw at work. Though I saw no reaction from my male counterparts, I could see some of the women's faces cloud with disapproval at her attire. Blair, my analyst, sat in the open chair between me and the President. The President finished his story to mild laughter around the room. Blair laughed and said, "Oh, great story, Dave! Should we get started?"

Complimenting the President and getting the meeting started without further delay was exactly the right thing to do. But when I stole a quick glance at the senior leaders around the room, I didn't see any appreciation for Blair taking the initiative. Instead, I saw a group of irritated forty- and fifty-year-olds. Each of them worked hard to get to be a direct report to the President, and they weren't very happy to see one of the business's youngest employees getting the spotlight.

Blair proceeded to walk us through an extremely insightful analysis. Her report clearly showed where our sales force was succeeding and where it was failing. It also provided leads for our sales reps to call on for new business. She was confident and articulate in her presentation—highlighting aspects of the analysis to the various leaders in the room. As she used their first names to direct their attention to a particular part of the report, the leaders would slowly lean back in their chairs and fold their arms. Their body language was sending a message—either they didn't like the presentation or they didn't like Blair. When she concluded her talk there was silence.

After a few moments that screamed "Awk–ward!" I asked, "So what do you guys think?"

A few grumbled "nice work" comments but that was it. The President continued the agenda and concluded the meeting. Then the parade to my door began ...

"What the hell was she thinking?" one sales leader started. "She shows up late, acts like she owns the place, and then tries to monopolize the entire meeting. I tried to help her out by asking a question, and she responded like she was my friend. I've been paying my dues here for 25 years—how dare she act like she's my equal. I saw her leave early on Friday, so she must not have put a ton of time into that analysis. In any case, she should have showed it to me before the meeting, so I could make some intelligent comments in front of the President."

The next few senior leaders through my doorway said essentially the same thing. Those conversations also included comments like, "You need to rein her in" and "She thinks she should be CEO tomorrow, and she's only been here a year."

Just when I thought the day's venting was over, Blair came into my office. She was just as frustrated as her older counterparts, but for different reasons.

"What the hell were they thinking? I've been busting my butt on this analysis for an entire week. I even worked late Friday night on this after I got home from my kickball game." (Author's note: No kidding—she actually played in an organized kickball league. But we digress.) "I got no feedback and no thanks for my work. This is the sort of thing that should get me promoted and instead it's like it's totally worthless. They're just intimidated because I'm young and have new ideas."

In the end, the older generation of senior leaders around that table was right ... and wrong. And so was Blair. It came down to perspective—a perspective, in this case, that was primarily driven by their generation. The Baby Boomers and Generation Xers who represented my company's leadership team were raised in a totally different environment and with parents who used completely different parenting techniques than Blair, my Millennial, was accustomed to.

Companies around the world are struggling with the same challenges. Up until about 1960, employees were good followers. They certainly had their own opinions, but as children of the Great Depression, they knew their job was sacred and directly followed the guidance of their business leaders. Likewise, as parents, this Mature generation expected their children to follow their orders without question. That strict parenting style had implications on their children, the Baby Boomers, and how the boomers raised their own children.

In the 1960s and 1970s, as the Baby Boomers came of age, they began questioning their parents' generation—free love, Vietnam War protests, fighting for racial equality—the Baby Boomers were willing to stand up for what they thought was right ... to a point. While protestors flooded the streets from Washington, DC, to San Francisco, *business* was still a game of follow the leader.

Take a minute to conjure an image of a business man in the 1960s. Chances are you came up with an image straight out of *The Right Stuff* or *The Graduate*—short hair, short-sleeve shirt with tie, perhaps even a pocket protector. There might have been hippies in the streets, but at IBM, you did what your leadership expected or you didn't have a job. Even in the 1970s as hair and sideburns got longer, there really wasn't a counterculture in business settings. If you did what you were told, you kept your job.

Then something happened. Businesses trying to meet Wall Street expectations and/or to achieve a profitability measure started to lay off employees. Employee attitudes changed. And employees passed these attitudes down to their children.

In the 1980s and '90s, employees no longer believed their employer would have a job for them. General employee lack of faith in company leadership didn't manifest itself in the form of protests in the workplace; there was still a clear line of distinction between what people were willing to protest outside of work versus inside, but attitudes clearly changed. Instead of following their leadership team with little obvious disagreement, employees started to question their management.

When previous generations were handed an assignment, a common response was, "Yes, sir." (There weren't too many women in leadership positions then, so it really was "yes, sir.") When Generation X was handed an assignment, however, the response was often to question authority: "Why is this important?" "How does this fit into our strategy?" "What if we did this differently and more efficiently?"

Imagine if you'd been saying "Yes, sir" your entire career and then, when you finally reach the level of a "sir," your subordinate questions your request. Grrrrrrr! Generation X had seen their parents get laid off, their peers laid off (or perhaps been laid off themselves), and just weren't willing to accept their leaders' directives at face value any longer. If businesses were no longer committed to their employees, then employees weren't going to commit their lives to their employer. At the same time, Generation X's parents were getting divorced at the highest rates in history. "Commitment" just didn't carry as much weight as it used to, and this affected Generation X at work and at home.

Growing up in single-parent homes (or with two parents who both worked), Gen X had to learn to fend for themselves after school. Known as "latch key children" (kids who had to let themselves into a locked house or apartment), Gen X was left to explore the notion of work/life balance. They'd learned that they couldn't count on their employer to take care of them and they couldn't necessarily count on their parents to be there all the time, so they became more self-centered. Work was a means to an end—not an end unto itself.

Michael Douglas's character, Gordon Gekko, in the 1987 film *Wall Street* told us, "Greed is good," and that sentiment became somewhat thematic of the 1980s. That's not to suggest everyone in Generation X is greedy, but they were (and remain) more individualistic than previous generations. Matures needed to work together to overcome the remnants of the Great Depression. Baby Boomers assembled publicly to share their displeasure with government policy. Gen X wasn't so sure they could count on others and so started thinking more about their own particular circumstances. That might mean working hard to get a fancy car or it might mean working enough to buy their children what they wanted/needed, but less and less it meant working hard to ensure the company got what it wanted.

As the younger Baby Boomers and then the Gen Xers became parents, they wanted to right the perceived wrongs of their parents. Gone was harsh performance feedback like, "If you keep that attitude, you'll never amount to anything." Instead, phrases like this were replaced by phrases like "If you do your best, you can accomplish anything." The vast majority of children in the Millennial generation (also known as Generation Y) were reminded on a nearly daily basis that they were "special." To reinforce this feeling of "specialness," every child who participated in a competition received the same participation trophy. "Every child should be made to feel special," proponents said.

You have to ask, though …

If every child gets the same trophy, how does that make them feel special?

We'll address that later in this book, but suffice it to say, Millennial children grew up expecting more out of life than at least their work life was prepared to give them. Remember how Gen X ruffled feathers by questioning authority? Imagine what older generations thought of employees who expected to be rewarded for each accomplishment.

In addition, the latest group of post Millennials, Generation Z, has a slightly different twist from the preceding generation. Whereas Gen X was shaped by their parents getting laid off and divorced, Gen Z was greatly influenced by the Great Recession. Another way to think about it is "Millennials" and "Millennials AL" (or "After Lehman"). Those children old enough to remember the fall of Lehman Brothers and many other firms and the impact it had on their parents' lives have an even smaller level of commitment—to their employer and to life in general. Plan to stay with one company for their entire career? No way. Plan to buy a house and hope they'll have the income to continue to make their payments? They're not so sure.

Remarkably, this generation is more willing than any previous one to get a permanent tattoo inked on a very visible body part that will affect their life and hire-ability forever. There's commitment there, just a very different sort of commitment than previous generations.

As you can see, each generation has their own history, perceptions, expectations, and approach to getting things done. It would be hard enough to have to lead a single generation beyond our own, but we've got a bigger challenge.

Due in large part to people living longer and the Great Recession wiping out the savings of older employees, members of the Mature and Baby Boomer generations are working longer, some well into their seventies. At the same time, according to the Pew Research Center, Millennials now represent the largest generation in the labor force (35 percent of employees).[13] That means we now have five generations in any given organization and each one has unique expectations, is motivated by different things, and has different goals. To complicate this scenario further, each generation could be a leader or a follower (or both). It's not just the older generation at the top of the organizational hierarchy any longer.

Millennials became the largest generation in the labor force in 2016

U.S. labor force, in millions

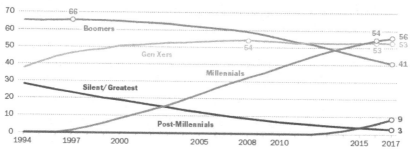

Note: Labor force includes those ages 16 and older who are working or looking for work. Annual averages shown.
Source: Pew Research Center analysis of monthly 1994-2017 Current Population Survey (IPUMS).
PEW RESEARCH CENTER

In order to succeed, leaders will have to understand how to get the most out of members of every generation by varying their approach and using specific techniques to recruit, train, manage, and inspire their employees. For those of you who do it right, your organization will be humming along on all cylinders. For those that do it wrong, you may be looking for your next job in the near future.

---

13. http://www.pewresearch.org/fact-tank/2018/04/11/millennials-largest-generation-us-labor-force/

CHAPTER 2

WHY A GOLDFISH

"If you change the way you look at things,
the things you look at change."

– Wayne Dyer

If you're not already familiar with Stan's series of "goldfish" books, you're probably asking, "What does a goldfish have to do with successfully leading different generations?" The answer may surprise you.

The origin of using goldfish as a metaphor dates back to 2009 with Gray Goldfish being the eighth color in the series. At its most basic level, the goldfish represents something small, but despite its initial size, it can grow to have a very powerful impact.

The first inspiration for the goldfish came from Kimpton Hotels. The boutique hotel chain introduced something new in 2001. The Hotel Monaco began to offer travelers the opportunity to adopt a temporary travel companion for their stay. Perhaps you are traveling on business and getting a little lonely. Or maybe you are with family and missing your family pet. Kimpton to the rescue; they will give you a goldfish for your stay. They called the program Guppy Love.

"The 'Guppy Love' program is a fun extension of our pet-friendly nature as well as our emphasis on indulging the senses to heighten the travel experience," says Steve Pinetti, Senior Vice President of Sales & Marketing for Kimpton Hotels and Restaurants, of which Hotel Monaco is part of their premier collection. "Everything about Hotel Monaco appeals directly to the senses, and 'Guppy Love' offers one more unique way to relax, indulge and promote health of mind, body and spirit in our home-away-from-home atmosphere."

The second part of our goldfish inspiration came from the peculiar growth of a goldfish. The average common goldfish is between three to four inches in length (ten centimeters), yet the largest in the world is almost six times that size! For comparison, imagine walking down the street and bumping into someone who is three stories tall.

How can there be such a disparity between regular goldfish and their monster cousins? It turns out the growth of the goldfish is determined by five factors. Just like goldfish, not all businesses grow equally, and we believe that the growth of a product or service faces the same five factors that affect the growth of a goldfish.

#1. SIZE OF THE ENVIRONMENT = THE MARKET

GROWTH FACTOR: The size of the bowl or pond.

IMPACT: Direct correlation. The larger the bowl or pond, the larger the goldfish can grow. Similarly, the smaller the market in business, the lesser the growth potential.

#2. NUMBER OF OTHER GOLDFISH IN THE BOWL OR POND = COMPETITION

GROWTH FACTOR: The number of goldfish in the same bowl or pond.

IMPACT: Inverse correlation. The more goldfish, the less growth. Similarly, the less competition in business, the more growth opportunity exists.

#3. THE QUALITY OF THE WATER = THE ECONOMY

GROWTH FACTOR: The clarity and amount of nutrients in the water.

IMPACT: Direct correlation. The better the quality, the larger the growth. Similarly, the weaker the economy or capital markets in business, the more difficult it is to grow.

> **FACT**
>
> A malnourished goldfish in a crowded, cloudy environment may only grow to two inches (five centimeters).

#4. THE FIRST 120 DAYS OF LIFE = STARTUP PHASE OR A NEW PRODUCT LAUNCH

GROWTH FACTOR: The nourishment and treatment received as a fry (baby goldfish).

IMPACT: Direct correlation. The lower the quality of the food, water, and treatment, the more the goldfish will be stunted for future growth. Similarly, in business, the stronger the leadership and capital for a start-up, the better the growth.

#5. GENETIC MAKEUP = DIFFERENTIATION

GROWTH FACTOR: The genetic makeup of the goldfish.

IMPACT: Direct correlation. The poorer the genes or the less differentiated, the less the goldfish can grow. Similarly, in business, the more differentiated the product or service from the competition, the better the chance for growth.

> **FACT**
>
> The current *Guinness Book of World Records* holder for the largest goldfish hails from The Netherlands at a whopping 19 inches (50 centimeters). To put that in perspective, that's about the size of the average domestic cat.

WHICH OF THE FIVE FACTORS CAN YOU CONTROL?

Let's assume you have an existing product or service and have been in business for more than four months. Do you have any control over the market, your competition, or the economy? NO, NO, and NO.

The only thing you have control over is your business's genetic makeup or how you differentiate. In goldfish terms, how can you lead your organization to stand out in a sea of sameness?

Now, why the color gray?

CHAPTER 3

WHY GRAY?

"It has long been an axiom of mine that the little things are infinitely the most important."

– Sir Arthur Conan Doyle

Hopefully, we've convinced you that a goldfish is a pretty good metaphor for how something small, if provided the right circumstances, can grow into something large and impactful. But why choose the color gray?

Unfortunately, there isn't always a clear-cut path to great leadership. In fact, there seldom is. When you couple this with leading people who, because of their generation, perceive the world very differently, there is no black and white approach to success. You'll have to use a variety of techniques to overcome challenges and get the most from your employees. A one-size-fits-all approach is a recipe for disaster because your employees approach their work differently. This holds true even for an organization with just one generation, much less one with five. You're going to have to navigate plenty of gray areas to find the approach that works best.

Likewise, gray is a color often associated with something nondescript or unremarkable. We hate to be the ones to tell you this, but that's how most employees view their leadership team. Forbes tells us that 63 percent of employees don't trust their leaders.[14] Gallup also completed a study saying a staggering 87 percent of employees are not engaged (and leadership plays at least a passing role in that).[15] In addition, Accor/Edenred states that 90 percent of companies think an engagement strategy will improve business success.[16] Yet, very few companies have a strategy. Is it because they don't want to be successful? Perhaps they're too lazy? Or maybe it's because they don't know how.

This book is going to provide you clear, actionable approaches to win over and engage every generation in your workforce, so you can create a strategy specific to your employees and your situation.

---

14. https://www.forbes.com/sites/christinecomaford/2017/01/28/63-of-employees-dont-trust-their-leader-heres-what-you-can-do-to-change-that/

15. https://www.gallup.com/services/190118/engaged-workplace.aspx

16. Reward to Engage 2008, Accor Services

We won't be addressing solutions regarding why you don't care to be successful and why you're too lazy. We're guessing you do and you're not.

Does it really matter if you engage all five generations of employees in your company? The Korn Ferry Institute would suggest it does. Their study determined that firms that engage and enable their employees achieve up to 4.5 times more revenue growth than companies that don't.[17] Kenexa echoed this stat, saying companies who have highly engaged employees earn twice the net income of companies that don't.[18]

Think about those stats. It doesn't matter if you're a small organization or a large one, doubling your revenue and net income is huge! And, if you want to create a new product or service, just connect with your employees—every generation, not just yours—so that they are engaged with their work. We're not telling you it's the easiest thing you'll ever do, but we guarantee it won't be the hardest.

---

17. https://www.kornferry.com/institute/employee-engagement

18. The Impact of Employee Engagement, Kenexa

CHAPTER 4

TALKING ABOUT MY GENERATION

"I hope I die before I get old."

– Pete Townshend from The Who, *My Generation*

Sorry, Pete Townshend, but you're old. The thing is, much of what shaped Pete's attitudes and approaches when he wrote that song continue to make him who he is today. It's the same for the members of each g-g-g-generation. (If you're a member of a generation that doesn't get why we just stuttered, listen to a sample of *My Generation* on your favorite streaming music platform. If you're from a generation that doesn't know how to stream music and also doesn't get the reference, shame on you.)

Before we get into how the generations were shaped, though, we need to define what groups we're talking about. Generally, the generations are:

GENERATION	BIRTH DATES
Matures	Prior to 1946
Baby Boomers	1946 – 1964
Generation X	1965 – 1979
The Millennials	1980 – 1996
Generation Z (The Post Millennials)	1997 – Present

As one would guess, not everyone fits exactly into these generational categories, but to a great extent they hold true. Some factors that alter the generational characteristics a little are the ages of the parents and where a child is born within the order of siblings. For instance, Mature parents may have a few children in the Baby Boomer generation and a couple in Gen X. Chances are those Gen X children were raised like (and exhibit some characteristics of) Baby Boomers.

In order to learn how to lead each of the generations, it's important to understand why each generation is the way it is. In other words, what's shaped their attitudes, approaches, and perspectives?

CHAPTER 5

MATURES

"If I do my full duty, the rest will take care of itself."

– General George S. Patton

P atton's quote sums up the Mature generation. They're about doing their job, taking care of business and not complaining. Why? Take a minute to think about growing up prior to 1946. The Matures (or at least their parents) lived through the worst economic times this country has ever seen. Check out these stats:

- Unemployment in 1933 was 25 percent.[19]

- Millions of people were homeless or living in "Hooverville" shanty towns (so many that it's tough to get an accurate count, but it would not be a stretch to say up to 5 percent of the U.S. population was homeless—that's about 10 times what it was in 2018).[20]

- The Dow Jones Industrial Average (a measure of the U.S. stock market average) lost nearly 90 percent of its value between 1929 and 1932. It didn't reach its previous peak until 1955—23 years later![21]

- The average American family income dropped 40 percent from 1929 to 1932.[22]

- An estimated 50 percent of children during the Great Depression did not have adequate food, shelter, or medical care.[23]

Each generation has experienced an economic downturn, but nothing like this. When families are struggling to feed themselves or find a place to live, parents have zero tolerance for hearing their children complain that they "never get to do anything fun!" Instead,

19. http://www.american-historama.org/1929-1945-depression-ww2-era/great-depression-facts.htm

20. http://www.stockpickssystem.com/the-great-depression/,https://www.census.gov/ library/publications/1933/compendia/statab/55ed.html

21. Economists Discuss 2009 vs. the 1930s." Augustana College. January 27, 2009

22. http://great-depression-facts.com

23. https://www.amazon.com/Children-Great-Depression-Russell-Freedman/dp/0547480350

children learn to live with very few creature comforts and to stretch what they have—food, clothes, toys—as far as they possibly can.

A quick story from Brian's childhood. Raised by Mature generation parents, Brian and his four siblings had to take an extra step when the jelly jar was "empty." "Empty" is in quotes because to the practiced eye of a Mature generation member, it wasn't really empty. Brian's mother would swirl water in the jar to get the last bits of jelly from the jar's sides and then put that sugar-water jelly on the bread. Then the jar was empty.

Do the math: a jar of jelly back then was maybe 50 cents. We'd already gotten about 40 servings out of the jar to the tune of 1.25 cents apiece. Now, we're swirling water around to get another half serving (if we're being generous). That means that the final effort that created a soggy piece of bread saved about half a penny. But, having been shaped by such an austere childhood, it was worth it to a member of the Mature generation.

World War II also had a tremendous shaping effect on the Mature generation. While the Vietnam War would have a big effect on the Baby Boomers, consider that in Vietnam, 2.7 million American military members fought in the conflict with 58,000 dying.[24] In World War II, 16.1 million Americans fought in the war and 416,000 died. For other countries, the numbers are even more staggering. Russia lost about 24 million people (military and civilian), Japan 2.1 million, and Yugoslavia, a small country, lost 446,000.[25]

With nearly 10 percent of the U.S. population fighting in the war, supplies and food were rationed, and women entered the workforce en masse for the first time. On the home front, World War II was a part of every American's life. "Duty, Honor, Country" were words

24. https://www.uswings.com/about-us-wings/vietnam-war-facts/

25. https://www.nationalww2museum.org/students-teachers/student-resources/research-starters/research-starters-worldwide-deaths-world-war

that defined the Mature generation. Not "duty, honor, country ... but I have to leave work early today because my son has a soccer game" like we'll see with later generations.

An example of the selflessness exhibited by the Matures can be seen in the Army Air Corps B-17 crews. During World War II, B-17 crews flew from England and bombed Germany. Remember, this is the early 1940s, so no night-vision goggles, no hiding behind the clouds, no high-tech fighter jets protecting them. These are rudimentary aircraft with ten crew members (although there was really only space for about five),[26] bombing an enemy that knew they were coming—during the day. For a period of time, about 25 percent of the bombers would be shot down on any given day.[27] The remaining pilots would return to England, go to bed, wake up the next day, and fly the same mission. Another 25 percent would get shot down, and the cycle would continue as reinforcements were added from the States.

Photo courtesy of WW II in Color[28]

If you're not from the Mature generation, did you read the last paragraph and think, "Yeah, that makes sense. I would have done

26. https://b17flyingfortress.de/en/details/die-besatzung/)

27. https://en.wikipedia.org/wiki/Boeing_B-17_Flying_Fortress

28. http://www.ww2incolor.com/dramatic/Boeing+B-17+shot+down+by+Flak_+_Germany_+1945_.html

that too." Probably not. Your response more likely was, "Not me, brother. They could get someone else to put their life on the line every day." (Ok–if you're not a Baby Boomer, you probably didn't use the word "brother" when you were answering that question, but you get the point.)

For a moment, juxtapose your daily commute with what the B-17 crews faced. Traffic during rush hour may be a total hassle, but it's really rare for someone to shoot at you on the way to work. Imagine if when you got to work, a portion of your coworkers had died the previous day doing the exact job you're doing. Then, the next day, even more died … *doing your job*. How long would you keep going back to work?

Even before the war, work was serious business to the Mature. In 1940, automaker Henry Ford fired someone on his assembly line when the person was "caught in the act of smiling" and then later "laughing with the fellows."[29] Ford said, "When we are at work, we should be at work. When we are at play, we ought to be at play." Things were a little different back then.

Matures grew up in, and were shaped by, an era that required selflessness and sacrifice. It was about a team working together to achieve a common goal. They expected selflessness and sacrifice of themselves, and they expected it of their children. Their children, though, turned out to have different expectations.

---

29. https://medium.com/personal-growth/fired-for-smiling-e8fd4a31db69

CHAPTER 6

BABY BOOMERS

"Retirement kills more people than hard work ever did."

– Malcolm Forbes

While Matures were influenced by very austere conditions, Baby Boomers grew up in an era of abundance. Known as the "Decade of Prosperity," the U.S. economy grew 37 percent in the 1950s, and by 1959, families had 30 percent more purchasing power compared to the beginning of the decade. Unemployment dropped as low as 4.5 percent.[30]

As a result of these economic conditions, Americans changed their spending habits. While there might still have been people putting water in jars to get the last bit of jelly, consumerism grew. There were 67 million cars on U.S. roads in 1958 compared to only 8 million in 1950.[31] A television in every household was a common sight. And much of this consumerism was driven by Americans willing to go into debt. Private debt doubled in the 1950s as people borrowed to buy houses, cars, and even fancy meals. The first credit card, The Diner's Club card, was introduced in 1950.[32]

Despite this increased consumerism, Matures still raised their children with a stricter approach than future generations. When fathers came home from work, they didn't drop everything to play with their children. In fact, here's a sample of *Housekeeping Monthly's* "The Good Wife's Guide" (see if you can spot what's changed since then).[33]

> Prepare yourself. Take 15 minutes to rest so you'll be refreshed when he arrives. Touch up your makeup, put a ribbon in your hair and be fresh-looking. He has just been with a lot of work-weary people.

> Clear away the clutter. Make one last trip through the main part of the house just before your husband

---

30. https://www.shmoop.com/1950s/economy.html
31. https://www.enotes.com/homework-help/approximately-how-many-cars-were-registered-1950s-468029
32. https://www.shmoop.com/1950s/economy.html
33. https://www.littlethings.com/1950s-good-housewife-guide/

arrives. Gather up schoolbooks, toys, paper, etc. and then run a dust cloth over the tables.

Prepare the children. Take a few minutes to wash the children's hands and faces (if they are small), comb their hair and, if necessary, change their clothes.

Children are little treasures and he would like to see them playing the part. Minimize all noise. At the time of his arrival, eliminate all noise of the washer, dryer or vacuum. Try to encourage the children to be quiet.

You may have a dozen important things to tell him, but the moment of his arrival is not the time. Let him talk first—remember, his topics of conversation are more important than yours.

Your goal: Try to make sure your home is a place of peace, order and tranquility where your husband can renew himself in body and spirit.

There is so much here to comment on, but we'll limit ourselves to themes. 1) Everything should be picked up and orderly. 2) The children should be quiet and respectful (and oftentimes in another room). 3) The father gets to talk about his day, and his wife and kids should listen patiently (because *"his topics of conversation are more important"*).

Does this sound anything like the natural state of households with children? Toys are undoubtedly scattered on the floor, the kids are releasing their energy after sitting in school all day, and everyone wants to share some important aspect of their day (at least until the kids become teenagers when every question is answered with a monosyllabic grunt). This means that despite the efforts of the perfect 1955 wife, the kids are not going to meet Dad's expectations.

And, in the 1950s, if you didn't meet Dad's expectations, he didn't patiently explain why he wanted his rules enforced or slowly count to three. Instead, he raised his voice and perhaps he or Mom delivered a spanking. (Millennials and Gen Z members, in the 1950s, it was accepted and perhaps even expected to hit your children to help them learn.) Children of Matures remembered this parenting style when they became parents and most vowed to do things differently. We see this in how the Millennials were raised—keep reading!

With this relative wealth, Baby Boomers became better educated and began to question authority and social norms. They protested the Vietnam war—imagine what the B-17-flying Matures thought of that—and fought for equal rights for women and minorities. The key here is the phrase "social norms." As mentioned earlier, there still wasn't a lot of authority challenging in work environments. Passed down from their parents, work remained a privilege. Boomers remained loyal to their employers (though not quite as loyal as Matures) and believed in putting in a full-day's work (or longer). Even now, Boomers are less likely to retire when they reach their mid-sixties. Some of that has to do with economic conditions and the state of their investment portfolio after the Great Recession, but much of it has to do with actually enjoying their work and taking pride in their career. And you don't have to look too closely to see that career pride on display.

Take a look around a Baby Boomer's office or den. What do you see hanging on the walls? We bet in an overwhelming number of cases you see trophies and plaques. Baby Boomers are defined by their work and are interested in telling you about it. In one case, a Boomer was proudly displaying a certificate on his office wall from a Microsoft course he completed. No sweat—it was probably a tough course, and he was proud of it. Upon closer inspection, though, the certificate was from 1990. That was before Windows! What—he was proud that he'd learned MS DOS? (Millennials and

Gen Z, that's when you used to have to type in commands to get your computer to do something instead of clicking on an icon.)

Further investigation uncovered several more Microsoft certificates of the 25 or so that were displayed, all from the early 1990s. Clearly, they were important to him, but it's unlikely that equivalent certificates would be displayed by Gen Xers or Millennials, even if they were relatively recent. It's just not their style.

So why are Boomers so interested in displaying their achievements? It's because those achievements represent the path the Boomers took to reach their current status. While results are important, it's the process and the dues that have been paid that produced those results that are most important.

Ask a Boomer about themselves and they'll tell you all about their job: what they do, the role they play within their company, how many people report to them, etc. After several minutes you may find out that they're married, have children, and perhaps a few hobbies. Or maybe they'll never get to that.

Likewise, if you ask a Boomer for career advice, they'll walk you through how they got to where they are today—in detail, with lessons learned. They'll speak of the various positions and steps they took to achieve their status. Short cuts, something younger generations are very interested in learning about, are for the weak. Boomers are proud of the fact that they paid their dues to get to where they are today.

The industry that most closely matches Baby Boomer ideals and ways of thinking is the airline industry. For airline pilots, the #1 criterion for getting hired is hours flying an aircraft. Not hand/eye coordination, not unique flying experiences, not even the ability to sound cool on the radio … the cut is made by whether or not a pilot has a certain number of hours in the pilot's chair.

Similar criteria are used for promotion. In comparison to the pilot's peer group, whoever has the most time with the company gets the opportunity to upgrade first. For upgrade, it doesn't even matter if the pilot has more or fewer hours—short flights, long flights—it doesn't matter. Again, talent, superior eyesight, working well with crewmates, or any other criteria are not considered—only time with the company. In fact, some of that time doesn't even have to be associated with working. Airline pilots are issued a line number when they're hired. That's where they reside in the pilot hierarchy. When people ahead of them retire, the pilot moves up in the hierarchy. This includes time when the pilot is taking a sabbatical for military reserve duty or to be a mortgage broker for a year (really, true story). Pilots move up the hierarchy just because they've been with the company longer.

For Generation X, Millennials, and Generation Z, this is a tough situation. Their natural style is not to wait patiently for a spot to open, especially when they think they are more talented than their older counterparts. For Baby Boomers, though, this hiring and promotion scheme makes sense: everyone should pay their dues, and when they have, they get promoted.

Another group that embraces Baby Boomer characteristics is the military. In lieu of placing plaques and awards on the wall (or sometimes in addition to), military personnel wear their awards on their chest. On the formal "business suit" uniform known as service dress, military personnel wear a ribbon for each major award they've received throughout their career. It's very Baby Boomer-ish.

In line with showing off their career via plaques and awards, it's important for Boomers to get the opportunity to show their knowledge to others. In business settings, the most frequent opportunity to show their knowledge is in meetings. Boomers appreciate the opportunity to get face time with the boss by highlighting their projects and the processes they undertook to work on those projects.

Stay late at work one night. What generation do you see the most on a standard night? We bet it's Baby Boomers. We'll also bet you see the Boomers outside their offices so it's a little more obvious they're working late. Defined by their work, Boomers don't mind staying late (even if it means sacrificing some family time), and they take advantage of the opportunity to show off that work ethic to their managers and coworkers. Staying late and working hard are badges of honor for Boomers but not so much for the generation that followed them.

CHAPTER 7

GENERATION X

"People were not meant to sit in cubicles staring at computer screens all day listening to eight different bosses drone on about mission statements."

– Peter Gibbons (portrayed by actor Ron Livingston) in the movie *Office Space*

Generation X can be cynical and even sarcastic. Why do these attractive, smart, loving people sometimes come across as negative (can you tell we're from Generation X)? It's because some major things that previous generations accepted as "givens" didn't hold true for Gen X.

The first major area that changed for Gen Xers compared to previous generations is marriage. The parents of Generation X divorced at a greater rate than any other generation before or since. It peaked in the late seventies and early eighties just as Gen X was growing up and would feel the greatest impact of their parents splitting up.[34] In total, about half of all children with parents married in the seventies saw them divorce—that's compared to 11 percent for children born in the fifties.[35] Interestingly, divorce rates continue to drop with Gen X and the Millennials. There are a variety of reasons why divorce rates spiked in the seventies and eighties, but the outcome of these divorces was that Gen X didn't view the concept of "commitment" as previous generations had.

As a result of more single-parent households, Generation X children came home to empty houses far more often than any other group of children. They were even labeled "latch key children" because of it. So, from an early age, Gen Xers learned to rely on themselves. They needed to create their own fun and take greater responsibility for their own well-being. Both of these attributes translated into the type of adults and employees they would become.

Remember how Matures held their job sacred? After the Great Depression, employees kept their head down, worked hard, and often stayed with the same company for their entire career. Likewise, while Baby Boomers were demonstrating in the street, they were generally compliant (with new ideas) in their work lives. Companies reinforced this behavior with pensions and retirement plans

---

34. http://stories.avvo.com/relationships/divorce/numbers-breakdown-divorce-generation.html
35. https://nationalaffairs.com/publications/detail/the-evolution-of-divorce

that rewarded employees based on longevity. Essentially, there were incentives for Matures and Boomers to stay with the same company that were congruent with their upbringing.

Generation X's situation was different. They not only saw the need to look out for themselves at home, they also started to see the need to look out for themselves at work as employment became less stable. Unlike previous generations, late Baby Boomers and Gen Xers saw lifelong employment with the same company end. By the end of 1982, unemployment reached nearly 11 percent—the highest since 1941.[36] Millions of workers who had counted on pensions, particularly in manufacturing industries like the auto makers and construction where unemployment reached 25 percent, were now left to fend for themselves. It's bad enough to lose your job, but it's even worse when you believed your employer would keep you employed until retirement age and then reward you for being a loyal employee. Disgruntled, unemployed parents shared their perceived betrayal with their children, and Gen X didn't forget.

Because of the lack of trust bred in this era of parental divorces and turbulent employment layoffs, Generation X began to question authority like no generation before it. They didn't necessarily publicly protest like the Baby Boomers did, but they didn't buy into the Baby Boomer philosophy of paying their dues with their employer in exchange for future rewards (and remember, Baby Boomers are their parents and bosses). They became impatient with the time it took to advance at their companies and started to look for new employment opportunities.

---

36. https://en.wikipedia.org/wiki/Early_1980s_recession_in_the_United_States

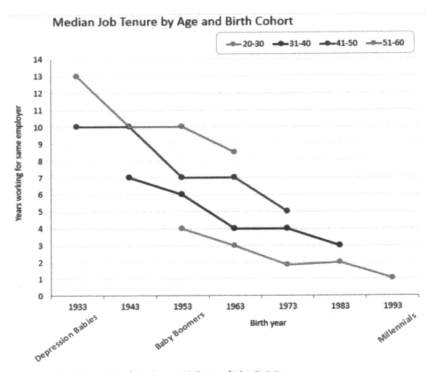

Median Job Tenure by Age and Birth Cohort

Source: Current Population Survey, U.S. Bureau of Labor Statistics

Even when generations are separated by their age at the time of a job change (younger people typically switch jobs more frequently than older people), the graph clearly shows how the average time working for the same company has plummeted from the Mature generation to Generation X.[37]

Gen X didn't just quit their jobs, though. They questioned authority within their existing employment—even in situations where you'd think everyone just accepted orders and did what they were told.

In 1997, a Korean Airlines 747 jet crashed into the mountainside in Guam three miles short of the runway killing 228 people. There

37. http://economistsview.typepad.com/economistsview/2015/06/falling-job-tenure-labor-as-just-another-commodity.html

were multiple warning system malfunctions that contributed to the disaster, but none of them affected the airplane's ability to fly. Beyond the systems, there was a large human component that led to the accident as well. Both the copilot and flight engineer noticed the plane (on autopilot with the Captain monitoring the controls) was descending sharply. Both were concerned that the plane was dropping below the recommended landing path, but neither spoke up. There was a culture within that cockpit that subordinates should not question the person in charge, and it ultimately resulted in a fatal crash.[38] This aligns with the Mature (and to a large extent, the Baby Boomer) generation's approach to work. Don't question authority.

For Gen X, however, this is completely counterintuitive. Allow the Captain to make a life-threatening mistake just so he can save face and you're not viewed as a trouble maker? No way! As an Air Force pilot, Brian's seen countless examples where Gen X junior officers spoke up even when a senior officer was at the controls. "Sir, I'm not going to let you kill me today," is an actual quote. While that statement likely rubbed the Baby Boomer senior officer the wrong way, it saved the crew, and the Gen X junior officer probably never hesitated to speak up.

In addition to questioning authority, Generation X was also the first generation to mix fun in business in earnest, and they made it known that they cared about their lives outside of work. Remember Henry Ford firing his employee for laughing on the job in the chapter about Matures? Gen Xers would never appreciate working for old Henry. They spawned work events like ping pong tournaments, riding skateboards, and the vending machine challenge. Never heard of the vending machine challenge? That's when an employee tries to eat one of everything in the office vending machine in one

---

38. https://www.washingtonpost.com/archive/politics/1998/03/18/is-culture-a-factor-in-air-crashes-guam-probe-may-raise-touchy-issue/7aca0396-a176-42ca-a4b0-4f6d8568115f/?utm_term=.ac0fac069316

8-hour day. Trying to consume thousands of calories and about 500 percent of the Recommended Daily Allowance of sodium in one day can be rough. The last time we saw a coworker attempt the feat, he sent periodic updates to the other employees who had pledged money if he finished the challenge. By eleven a.m., he reported, "I'm starting to feel dizzy. I need to slow down." By two p.m., he was done after having gone through about half of the items in the machine. We've never actually seen anyone finish the challenge, but it's fun to watch them try!

The introduction of Generation X in the workplace also coincided with casual dress in the office. In the seventies, nearly every employee in an office environment wore a suit and tie or female equivalent. With Gen X in managerial roles that transitioned to shorts and flip flops at many information technology companies. More conservative companies moved to khakis and polo shirts with jeans on Friday.

Not only did Gen X try to infuse fun into the workplace but they also represented the first group of workers who wanted work/life balance. Matures as products of the Great Depression were/are very hesitant to do anything that might put their employment in jeopardy. Baby Boomers personally identify with their jobs, so they don't have a great desire to leave work before all the tasks are finished. They also don't want to get the reputation as someone who leaves early or misses out on face time with the boss. Generation X, raised by those generations, wants to be more involved with their children's upbringing.

Remember when you ask Baby Boomers about themselves and they tell you all about the work and career? Brian asked a Gen X friend of his he hadn't seen in 15 years what he'd been up to. "I'm a hockey coach!" he proudly announced. He then went into some detail about how he needs to make split-second decisions while coaching. "Hockey?" We didn't have a hockey team at our high school (in southern California). "When did you learn to play? How'd you get to be a professional hockey coach?" Brian asked. "Oh, I'm not a professional coach," he replied. "I coach my son's hockey team. He's seven, and I learned the rules by reading articles online during my lunch hour at work." Turns out he does something totally different for a living. Sprinkle in a little cynicism and questioning of authority and he's a good example of Generation X. He defines himself by activities outside of work, spends more time with his kids than his father did, and tries to mix his work with his fun.

CHAPTER 8

THE NEW PEOPLE

I watch the ripples change their size
But never leave the stream
Of warm impermanence
And so the days float through my eyes
But still the days seem the same
And these children that you spit on
As they try to change their worlds
Are immune to your consultations
They're quite aware of what they're goin' through

Ch-ch-ch-ch-changes
Turn and face the strange
Ch-ch-changes
Don't tell them to grow up and out of it
Ch-ch-ch-ch-changes

– David Bowie, from the song *Changes*

When the Baby Boomers started to apply for college and enter the workforce, the Matures thought they were crazy. Peace, love, rock 'n' roll? Are you kidding me? These people will never amount to anything. Somehow, though, over time, the Matures started to accept the Baby Boomers and learned to work with them. At least the Boomers became serious about their work.

When Generation X applied for college and entered the workforce, the Matures and Boomers were in for another culture shock. These new employees were questioning the way things were being done. The Matures and Boomers had been successfully running business their way for decades, and these snot-nosed kids began coming in and suggesting changes. And having the audacity to leave at five (or earlier), because they had to take their kids to soccer practice or something. Not only that, but there was negative attitude. And women who wanted to work and have a family too! Somehow, though, Generation X proved itself to the Matures and Baby Boomers. It turned out some of their ideas were good ones, and they really did work hard with long hours—just not always from nine to five.

Then the Millennials entered the workforce and will soon be the largest working generation. This has prompted all three of the older generations to say, "What the *heck* (or something more colorful)!" These kids don't want to work, they think they're special, and they want to be promoted tomorrow. Just like the other generations, though, they bring a lot of new ideas and energy—it's just a matter of understanding how to direct those ideas and energy.

And it starts with understanding why the Millennials are the way they are.

CHAPTER 9

MILLENNIALS

*"My generation is zero.
I never made it as a working-class hero."*

– 21st Century Breakdown, Green Day

The Millennial approach to life starts with expectations. While previous generations met with hard times early in their lives (especially the Matures with the Great Depression and World War II and Generation X with divorces and layoffs), the Millennials have had some pretty good times up to this point. To illustrate that, take a look at savings rates up to 2006—two years before the start of the Great Recession.

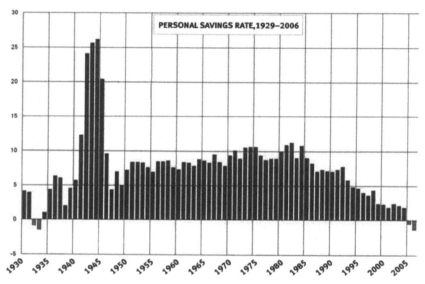

PERSONAL SAVINGS RATE, 1929–2006

This graph shows the percent of family income saved.[39] In the early thirties during the Great Depression, savings rates were negative. People spent more than they earned. Since unemployment was 25 percent, that seems pretty reasonable. From there, the country went to war. Supplies were rationed and people couldn't spend money even if they wanted to. When the soldiers returned from Europe and the Pacific, they had babies (hence the Baby Boomer generation) and increased spending while still saving. They made up for some lost time (figuratively and literally) and savings rates

---

39. http://bigpicture.typepad.com/comments/2006/06/james_altucher_.html

dropped. Within a few years, however, the savings rate in the U.S. started to increase.

Even though savings rates increased, plenty of money was still being spent. Home ownership for the average family became a reality. People purchased family cars and TV sets (sometimes even *color* TV sets!) Vacations become a little more extravagant. Then in 1983, even when more families than ever had dual incomes, savings rates started to drop.

While families used to have one car, they now had a car for each driver. While they used to have a family TV, they now had a TV in every bedroom. Camping trips to the state park became hotel stays in Europe or the Caribbean. Children had video games (and with the speed at which technology advanced, those video games got upgraded every couple of years.) Children had laptop computers and cell phones. Several years ago, Brian was at the park with his son when a 10-year old (at most) slid down the slide in front of him. He stayed seated at the bottom of the slide, reached into his pocket, and pulled out a cell phone. He then checked his messages while sitting on the slide. Times were changing.

Even families that were somewhat financially challenged spent money on their children like never before. Until finally, in 2006 and 2007, savings rates become negative again. Unlike during the thirties, there was no Great Depression—just a desire to spend more money (and some would argue a lack of discipline).

Besides the start of the decline in savings rates, what does 1983 represent? It represents the earliest memory of the Millennial generation. Psychologists tell us that much of a person's personality is developed by the time a child is seven years old. So, for the early Millennial generation, their personalities were developed in a period of ever-increasing spending. This sort of spending by their parents makes the Millennials expect more from their new parent-figures (their college professors and their managers at work). Since professors and managers have a different idea of what's expected of Millennials, these differing expectations set the Millennials up for disappointment.

Adding to their already high expectations, Millennials became the generation of trophy kids. If there was a children's race or other athletic event, more often than not, the first-place winner received a trophy. So what? This was how it had been for the other generations as well. Here's the difference: with the Millennials, second place got a trophy too. And third place ... and fourth place ... and fifth place ... and last place. Building self-esteem became the #1 priority of Millennial parents.

The concept of everyone getting a trophy didn't end with childhood either. Duke University professor Cathy Davidson[40] began letting her students grade themselves in her "This is Your Brain on the Internet" course. She argued that students work harder knowing they will be judged by their peers and ultimately end up learning more. Care to guess what grades students received from their classmates? Surprise! Everyone received an "A." You could contend that Professor Davidson is exactly right in her process for assessing students, or you could argue that she is completely wrong—she's received feedback on both ends of the spectrum. What you'll likely not argue is that this approach is far different from anything teachers have used in the past.

There is a variety of reasons why building their children's self-esteem was important for Millennial parents, but we would submit that the largest driving force was their own parents. For good or for bad, and as mentioned earlier, Mature and early Baby Boomer parents were not "touchy feely." Dads didn't rush home from work to play with their kids. They came home from work, got a drink,

---

40. News and Observer, June 20, 2010

and either turned on the news or talked with their spouse. They'd grown up in hard times and believed the discipline and toughness they developed were the key to their success in life. Therefore, they wanted to pass on that toughness to their kids by not making them "soft." Unfortunately, the majority of those children didn't appreciate the Matures' "tough love" and chose a different path when they became parents.

At the opposite end of the "tough love" spectrum are overly involved parents. Instead of ignoring their children or patting them on the head and telling them "now go and play," the parents of Millennials were (and in many cases, still are) in nearly constant contact with their children. It wasn't unique for Millennials' parents to text or call their children throughout the day to see how things were going, to check in on important events, and to provide guidance.

As an Admissions Officer for the Air Force Academy, Brian gets to mentor and evaluate high school students who want to attend the prestigious school. It's in this role that he also hears some surprising stories. In one case, Brian asked a very well-qualified student if he had brought his resume along with him to the evaluation interview. The student replied, "Yes. My parents worked on it last night so it should be good." Two immediate thoughts: 1) How odd that the student's parents worked on this resume for him. 2) How odd that he said that out loud.

Sometimes the level of parental involvement is too much to let go. One student at the Air Force Academy—after a one-year application process—quit after only a few weeks. Her reason? The Academy took her cell phone away at the beginning of basic training (as they did with everyone else), and she couldn't handle being out of touch with her parents for so long. We're not kidding. The equivalent of a $400,000 scholarship and guaranteed job were abandoned because a college student needed to be in daily contact with her parents.

These consistently hovering "helicopter parents" (no Air Force pun intended), don't limit themselves solely to parent/child interactions either. Starting in the mid two-thousands, it became somewhat common for parents to be involved in choosing their children's college courses and not just at the dinner table when reviewing options. Academic advisors at multiple colleges have shared how parents attend academic track meetings with their child and the advisor, choosing the classes the student will take. In addition, according to the *Chronicle of Higher Education,* parents have "become very active in calling or e-mailing their children's professors as well as college administrators and staff with their concerns. The *Chronicle* is now publishing guidelines for how schools should manage the parents of Millennials.[41]

As Millennials entered the workforce, their parents continued to stay involved. The *Wall Street Journal, Huffington Post,* and others report that 31 percent of Millennials had a parent apply for a job on behalf of their child, 8 percent brought their parents with them to a job interview, and 3-4 percent actually had their parents sit in on the job interview.[42] If you're from one of the generations not involved here, you'd think this was crazy or at least embarrassing, but that's far from the truth. In fact, after a keynote at a company's headquarters on this very topic, a Millennial approached Brian to share that his father had applied for the job he currently held with that particular company "while I ate a big bowl of cereal." What made the scenario even harder to believe was that the Millennial's manager was also queued up to speak with Brian. The manager, from Generation X, called him out on it. "You're actually telling that story right now? I'm standing right next to you!" The Millennial replied, "Yeah, sorry, but it's the truth. Big ol' bowl of Cap'n Crunch." The manager later shared that while shocked at his employee's

41. https://www.chronicle.com/article/Managing-Millennial-Parents/130146
42. https://www.huffingtonpost.com/2013/09/11/parent-job-interview_n_3907447.html, https://work.qz.com/1175864/parents-stop-butting-in-to-your-millennial-kids-job-searches/

revelation, the employee was one of his best, and he wouldn't be holding this story against him.

Why would a Millennial be so emboldened as to share a story like this? For one, it's so common for Millennials' parents to be involved in their lives that they don't even think twice about sharing that involvement with others. All their friends had involved parents, so they've grown up thinking it's normal. Secondly, Millennials were raised to have very high self-esteem and to believe their actions are the right ones.

From an early age, Millennials were told they were special. That, if they put their mind to it, they could be anything they wanted to be. Seems reasonable, doesn't it? In fact, we once heard a corporate coach describe how he started the mantra, "You ... have unlimited potential" with his children the day they were born. And he told them that every day of their life (until, we assume, they became teenagers and stopped listening to him). Brian's oldest son was very young at the time, so he adopted the mantra for him. Each day when he drove him to day care, he would tell him, "You have un-limited potential." After a while (and his son was able to talk), Brian would ask, "Did you know you have unlimited potential?" And his son would answer, "Yeesss ..." in that tone that kids reserve for a situation when you proved to them that you were right and they were wrong. It was during that time that we started to research the different generations and how the Millennials were raised. And we reached a crossroads.

Our research told us that as Millennials entered the workforce, most of them realized they were no longer treated as special. Their managers treated them like every other employee (at best) or as new people who didn't know anything. "How can this be?" they thought. "My mom and dad, whom I love dearly and despite all their faults were pretty smart, told me I was special. This stupid manager isn't appreciating me and all my special qualities." Once that first wave of frustration subsided, the Millennials turned to the other mantra they'd heard throughout their life—they "put their mind to it" so they could be anything they wanted to be.

Alas, concentrating hard and applying themselves at work did not always produce the recognition they sought. Some were fantastic and rose above their peers. Many, however, were (gasp!) average. Others still were (double gasp!) ... below average. It's a depressing time when you thought you were one thing and it turns out you're something less. It's even more depressing when you realize you're going to be that "less" thing you didn't think you were for the rest of your life.

Even the concept of being "special" could be the subject of ridicule. While to a Millennial, being special was a compliment and indicative of endless possibilities, it is not viewed that way by older generations. When Generation X hears someone called "special," they think of a mental or physical disadvantage—like the Special Olympics. For the Baby Boomers and Matures, being called "special" is an insult. As in, "What do you think you are ... special?!" The Millennials had entered a world that was very different from what they'd experienced in high school, college, and at home. And it didn't feel good.

Which brings us back to the crossroads parents faced. They wanted their children to believe they could be anything they wanted to be. Professional athlete, actor, racecar driver, astronaut—anything. After all, though we rose through the ranks of our respective careers, we spent a good portion of our later years making PowerPoint slides. In fact, Brian still does (but let's not talk about that because it makes him cry.) Do we really want our children thinking that if they get a good education, they will have the opportunity to make PowerPoint slides? That's a rhetorical question, but we'll answer it anyway—"No f&^%ing way!" Parents across the world struggle with the same dilemma. In the meantime, we have a generation whose current environment is not living up to their expectations.

Dr. Polly Young-Eisendrath wrote a thoughtful book titled, *The Self-Esteem Trap*[43] where she points out how, in an effort to raise confident children, we're also setting them up for failure. If you'd like to learn more about this phenomenon, check out this book. The impact of this disconnect can be devastating.

While Millennials were raised believing anything was possible, the generation that followed them, Generation Z, saw the results of a market collapse and a struggling economy and that produced lower expectations and even less desire to make a commitment, especially to an employer.

43. https://www.amazon.com/Self-Esteem-Trap-Confident-Compassionate-Self-Importance/dp/0316013129

CHAPTER 10

GENERATION Z

"Life is like the monkey bars: you have to let go to move forward. Once you make the decision to leap ..., be sure to loosen your grasp on old concepts so you can swing your way to new ones."

– Leah Busque, Founder, TaskRabbit

Generation Z, a.k.a. the post Millennials or Millennials A.L. (for "After Lehman"), is just beginning to enter the workforce, and it's critical to understand their unique perspective. Will they just be an extension of the Millennials? Early indications are a resounding "No!"

Born in 1997 or later, Generation Z is old enough to have felt the impact of the Great Recession of 2008-2012 with unemployment reaching 10 percent and much higher figures when you combine unemployment with underemployment (a stat that's much harder to measure). The lack of income forced Gen Z parents to draw down their savings. At the same time, the global stock markets dropped significantly. The U.S. S&P 500, Dow Jones Industrial Average, and NASDAQ markets all lost over 50 percent of their value from fall 2007 to spring 2009.[44] The net effect was a rapid reduction in retirement nest eggs and household cash flow.

Likewise, in the 18 months from December 2007 to June 2009, four million homes were foreclosed upon and another eight million foreclosures were started.[45] Because there were so many homes on the market and many at reduced prices, home values also dropped significantly—33 percent nationwide and as high as 60 percent in certain areas like Nevada.[46]

"Wait!" you say. While these conditions greatly affected the parents of Generation Z, what's all this got to do with their children? The answer: a lot. Remember how the spending habits of Millennial parents affected their children's expectations? So, too, did the belt tightening of the childhood and teenage years of Gen Z. Between loss of income and stock market investments, the median family's net worth dropped 40 percent during the Great Recession with only 38 percent of families in 2012 thinking they could live comfortably

---

44. https://en.wikipedia.org/wiki/United_States_bear_market_of_2007%E2%80%9309
45. https://projects.ncsu.edu/ffci/publications/2012/v17-n1-2012-spring/bennett.php
46. https://www.housingwire.com/articles/42654-corelogic-housing-market-nearly-recovered-from-recession

once they retired.[47] It doesn't take an economist to figure out that when people are concerned about their income and savings, they spend less money. They also impart their lessons learned to their children. Conversations with children about how Mom lost her job and Dad lost 50 percent of his money in the stock market become more common, and the children absorbed these lessons. And even if Gen Z's parents didn't sit them down for a talk, the reduction in Christmas presents, vacations, and restaurant dinners did the talking for them.

Having seen what happened to their parents' employment, Gen Z has started to look for other ways to make a living. Unlike Generation X, who generally continued to toe the corporate line despite seeing their parents laid off (they were just bitter about it), Gen Z is embracing the rise of the "gig" economy. We've seen a significant rise in shared services over the last decade and while shared cars (Car2go, Zipcar), shared rides (Uber, Lyft), and easy-to-access marketing support (Fiverr) may feel new to older generations, it's just how business gets done for Gen Z.

Gen Z also sees work commitment as a two-way street; if companies aren't willing to commit to their employment, why should they commit to a company? As evidence, 61 percent of high school students in 2014 said they would prefer being an entrepreneur and that belief has carried over into their college and early-work years.[48] Coupled with Gen Z's perception that they can't count on a single employer, they also embrace the flexibility being a contractor affords them. This approach has significant implications on how organizations need to think about gaining and retaining their youngest employees.

You'll remember from earlier that Baby Boomers love face time with senior leadership. And they are willing to stay late to get it.

---

47. http://money.cnn.com/2017/12/01/news/economy/recession-anniversary/index.html
48. https://www.entrepreneur.com/article/231048

Now Baby Boomers often *are* the senior leaders of their respective companies and assume their employees should want what they always wanted, including after-hours time for a chance to see the boss. "If I can't see you working, then you're probably not," is common refrain from Baby Boomer managers. Gen Z sees the world very differently.

As true digital natives, people who have never known life without a smartphone and instant connectivity to information, it seems insane to be tied to a desk from nine to five. It's not a lack of motivation, it's a lack of understanding as to why someone should work for eight to ten hours straight and then completely disconnect for the other fourteen to sixteen hours of the day. While other generations thought of work/life balance, Gen Z thinks about work/life *integration*. They don't want to work constantly (no one does), and they get that they can't play all day, but it doesn't make sense that the difference between work and play needs to be so delineated. Especially when they can perform many (sometimes all) of their job functions from home (or a coffee shop).

The idea of wanting to be an entrepreneur also influences how Gen Z wants to be supervised. While the Millennials were raised believing if they put their mind to it, they could achieve anything, Gen Z had a greater dose of reality. They saw their parents go through hard times and are aware that sometimes even smart people need help. They don't want to be micromanaged. In truth, no generation really appreciated that, and the Baby Boomers were the last to tolerate it. Gen Z, however, does realize they don't know everything. Instead of a manager, they want a mentor.

In a survey of 5,000 members of Generation Z by Door of Clubs, "37 percent of respondents noted health care benefits were the most important benefit, closely followed by a mentorship program

(33 percent)."[49] We're pretty sure Generation X didn't even know what mentorship was until they started working!

This creates a three-way challenge for managers. Gen Z has had a lot of parental involvement in their homework and other activities. Not as much as the Millennials, but far more than previous generations. Like the Millennials, this means that when they show up to for their first (or 100th) day of work, they have less project management experience than their managers had at the same age. That's challenge #1.

The second challenge is that many Gen Z employees are managed by members of Generation X, a generation that is used to working alone and typically doesn't feel the need to become actively involved in their subordinates' projects. All things being equal, Generation X would like to give their employees the freedom they enjoy: don't micromanage me; just tell me what needs to be done and let me do it. On top of this, Generation X is a stickler for efficiency, and every moment spent holding their employees' hands is a moment they aren't able to do their own job.

Finally, as previously shown, Gen Z wants to be mentored, not managed. So, put yourself in the shoes of a Generation X manager for a moment.

Your Gen Z employees don't know how to manage projects on their own.

You don't want to spend a lot of time with them.

They don't want to be managed; they want you to mentor them through a career in your organization.

---

49. https://www.doorofclubs.com/z

This isn't an easy situation, but all is not lost. While Gen Z is not the greatest at managing projects (at least when they first get to work), they are good at experimenting to find answers.

Think about the last time you bought some kind of machine. Not a service or food but a phone, kitchen appliance, computer, lamp, etc. Now think about the instructions that came with it. Aside from the legally-obligated picture and short paragraph in 18 languages that says, "Don't eat this or put it in a full bathtub with you," there really aren't any instructions, are there? Even when you're putting together a piece of furniture, the instructions are all graphic and pretty limited (and we're pretty sure the manufacturer never includes all the pieces you need, but that's for another book).

Older generations can remember when everything came with detailed instructions, but Gen Z can't. Ever since they could read, purchases didn't come with instructions. They required people to basically figure out the solution on their own. And that's where Gen Z excels.

When Gen Z gets a new phone, they play with it until they've figured out everything they need to know. Say all you want about this generation being lazy, but they will focus—with joy—until they've solved the problem they want to solve. And if they can't solve it on their own, they quickly engage their peers to help them solve it. Be advised, they won't call their peers so you won't hear them engaging their peers; it'll happen electronically. Rest assured, though, they will work doggedly until they've solved the issue.

As a young child, Brian's older son, Nick, wasn't much of a reader. He'd enjoy having books read to him but wasn't one to flip through picture books picking out the few words he knew until he learned how to read. It wasn't until he had a challenge to overcome that he really put his mind to reading. The challenge? How to watch his shows on TV.

Brian and his wife, Heidi, recorded Nick's shows on the digital video recorder (DVR) and would play them for him when he (or they) were ready for some downtime. The challenge was how to watch the shows when Mom and Dad weren't around. Without instructions, Nick used trial and error with "The List" on the DVR to identify his shows and then learned what letters spelled the names of the shows he wanted to watch. This was at age two. When Nick started preschool, the teachers raved about his reading ability and applauded Heidi and Brian for the time they had clearly spent with him teaching him to read. Brian accepted this praise with silent grace; Heidi quickly excused herself from the conversation.

Like every generation, Gen Z brings leadership challenges with it, but also unique abilities and characteristics that can elevate organizations. The key with all generations is to utilize and grow these abilities while incorporating employees from every generation into the fabric of your organization.

We all see and hear about the bad situations:

"Ugh – I've brought in some Matures to leverage their knowledge, but they're so gruff. They can't understand why I want to take care of outside-work tasks during the day. I'll get my work done, just on my time."

"Ugh – We've tried to nudge our Baby Boomers to non-leadership roles, but they're so resistant. I can't get promoted if they won't leave, and they always want to tell me exactly how to do my job. And worse yet, they want to *see* me do my job."

"Ugh – I've tried to mentor my best Generation X employees so they can take over when I leave, but they don't seem to be invested in our organization. They just want to do their job and move along. I can't get them to engage."

"Ugh – I know my Millennials have great ideas so I'm trying to involve them in bigger projects, but they have such high expectations. If they don't get to lead something monumental in a matter of weeks, they quit and move on to the next job. I can't get them to focus."

"Ugh – We're excited about what Generation Z brings to the table, but they try to do things their own way from minute one. Why can't they follow the rules we've been using for the last decade?"

When focusing on the bad examples, though, all we learn is how not to do things. We've found it's a better use of time to focus on good examples, so regardless of your situation, you'll have at least a few different techniques you can try out to engage every generation you lead. That's what's next.

PART II

NAVIGATING
THE GRAY

We crowdsourced 220 examples on List.ly as part of the Gray Goldfish Project.[50] The objective was to find real world examples of leading across the generations. Through our research and third-party submissions, we began to see patterns. Eight different themes emerged. We have listed them based on the progression of the employee lifecycle:

- Recruiting and Onboarding

- Vision and Purpose

- Training and Development

- Flexing

- Project Management

- Recognition and Motivation

- Feedback and Mentoring

- Retention and Loyalty

We'll share 50 ideas in Part II to get you thinking about ways to improve employee experience and help you lead across the generations.

Let's get started with recruiting and onboarding ...

---

50. https://list.ly/list/29T1-gray-goldfish-list

CHAPTER 11

RECRUITING AND ONBOARDING

"The way you manage the transition
of somebody into your culture speaks volumes
about the culture to the person coming in,
because you're making those first early impressions
and they know what's expected of them."

– George Bradt

Research shows that employees make the critical decision to stay or leave within the first six months on the job. When new hires participate in an effective recruiting and onboarding process, leaders can maximize retention, engagement, and productivity. Getting it right across the generations leads to higher job satisfaction, better job performance, and a reduction in stress.

Having a diverse range of ways to recruit, onboard, and retain a new hire is critical to establishing a healthy employer-employee relationship. Here we'll share 17 companies that purposefully go the extra mile to engage new team members across the generations.

This chapter is broken up into two sections: recruiting and onboarding.

RECRUITING

Let's first look at recruiting.

1. PARENT ACT IN RECRUITING

Unlike previous generations, Millennials and Generation Z look to their parents for guidance when considering job opportunities. Knowing this, the **U.S. Army** started a new approach to recruiting in 2010. As part of a video series, they encouraged recruits to sit down with their parents and discuss why they wanted to join the military. At the same time, the Army created a section on their website appealing to parents. Here was the tagline they used, *"You made them strong. We'll make them Army strong."*

General Mills was recently trying to recruit a high potential candidate out of college. Knowing he would have numerous job offers and that he would consult his mom and dad in the decision-making process, General Mills focused on convincing the whole family. The week before Thanksgiving, a turkey arrived at the house, accompanied by a Betty Crocker's Cookbook. According to Lynne Lancaster and David Stillman in *When Generations Collide*, "Betty's recipe was a winner when the student accepted the job offer a few weeks later. Whatever way you choose to do it, it is possible to create momentum even before a new person pulls in the parking lot."[51]

Keeping it open. **Enterprise Rental Car** uses open house events to recruit parents of Millennials. While their recruiting efforts apply to Millennials directly, they've found that the parents have so much influence on their children, they can be successful by recruiting the parents. The rental car company asks prospective employees if they'd like an info packet mailed to their parents. According to the book *Generations at Work*, most applicants accept the offer.[52] Authors Ron Zemke, Claire Rainers, and Bob Filipczak also share how **Merrill Lynch** has adopted a similar strategy. Recruiting efforts weren't working because candidates thought the job meant long hours and big demands at the firm. Merrill found that some of that perception was coming from parents. "They now have a Parents' Day where parents learn about the company, its benefits, the way business is done, and how employees are supported. Success rates have been huge."[53]

2. THINK BEYOND BROCHURES

Blue Cross Blue Shield of North Carolina has figured out a way to engage younger employees when recruiting. They recently launched a virtual reality experience whereby job seekers can take a virtual tour of the impressive Durham campus at job fairs.

51. https://www.amazon.com/When-Generations-Collide-Clash-Generational/dp/0066621070

52. https://www.amazon.com/Generations-Work-Managing-Boomers-Workplace/dp/0814432336

53. https://www.amazon.com/Generations-Work-Managing-Boomers-Workplace/dp/0814432336

3. ATTRACTING BOOMERS AND BOOMERANGERS

According to AARP, 4 of 10 workers over age 65 plan to continue working compared with about 1 in 10 less than 3 decades ago. **Wahve** is a contract staffing firm that specializes in recruits over 50 with roles spanning from CFO to sales associate. They like Boomers who are "pre-retiring" because they tend to stay in their role longer (average tenure of 10 years versus 2.8 for Millennials) and have more connections. Similarly, the accounting firm **PKF O'Connor Davies** actually seeks out and hires senior accountants who have aged out at other firms. According to the *Wall Street Journal*,[54] the firm leverages their experience to mentor associates in addition to their other responsibilities. Those senior folks tend to stay five years on average.

Because **E&Y** can bill more for experienced pros, they want to have more of them. They've created an alumni program that keeps in touch with 32,000 former employees. The alumni participate in workshops, volunteer events, and networking sessions. According to the book *Generations at Work*, of all the people who left E&Y, 28 percent have returned to the firm.[55]

ONBOARDING

The formal transition process for new employees is called onboarding. Here's how it is defined:

Onboarding, also known as organizational socialization, refers to the mechanism through which new employees acquire the necessary knowledge, skills, and behaviors to become effective organizational members and insiders. Tactics used in this process include formal meetings, lectures, videos, printed materials, or

---

54. https://www.wsj.com/articles/one-accounting-firm-wants-to-hire-retirees-1516201200
55. https://www.amazon.com/Generations-Work-Managing-Boomers-Workplace/dp/0814432336

computer-based orientations to introduce newcomers to their new jobs and organizations.[56]

Unfortunately, fewer than 25 percent of organizations have a formal onboarding process. According to onboarding pioneer and expert George Bradt, "Most organizations haven't thought things through in advance. On their first day, [new employees] are welcomed by such confidence-building remarks as: Oh, you're here. We'd better find you an office."

Culturally onboarding new hires can be a real challenge. While sleek videos, laminated pocket cards, and lobby placards may help employees memorize the company values, the actual understanding of how to "live" the company values can be a whole other story.

4. FIRST IMPRESSIONS MATTER

Attitudes begin to form at the initial point of contact with an organization. There is no better place to start than when you are welcoming new employees to your company. As the saying goes, "You never get a second chance to make a first impression." According to Lynne Lancaster and David Stillman in *When Generations Collide*:

> Regardless of the content of a formal orientation, companies miss an opportunity if they are not taking advantage of the impression made by efforts before the new employee shows up the first day. Imagine a Mature receiving a handwritten note from the CEO containing a simple and heartfelt welcome. Or a Boomer's family invited to attend a plant tour on family day. Or an Xer receiving a package containing

---

56. https://en.wikipedia.org/wiki/Onboarding

a company sweatshirt and a cap—and an invitation to join the softball team.[57]

At **Twitter**, all new hire desks are strategically placed next to the vital team member that they will be working with most from day one. Not to mention that each new employee is greeted with a T-shirt, a bottle of wine, and a customized email address. To add to the fun of the first day jitters, Twitter's CEO eats breakfast with all new hires, takes them on a tour of the company space, and ends the day with group program training specific to each person's new role.[58]

5. THE BUDDY SYSTEM

Asana sets up a desk and computer in advance and provides $10K for further customization for their new hires. The most common customization choice is a sweet motorized desk that allows a person to sit or stand to work just by hitting a button (because we all know stand-up desks can save your life). The workspace customization is just one step in the onboarding process for developers at Asana. The company also assigns each new employee a buddy. A co-worker with tenure gets assigned to the new developer. In addition to helping the new hire get settled in, the buddy schedules a series of learning sessions on various engineering topics over the first few weeks.

Capital One runs a Buddy Assimilation program. Buddy Assimilation matches veterans with newcomers. "Buddies" show the newbies around, have lunch with them, and act as a resource. After a month of training, new employees work "in the nest" for two weeks fielding incoming calls with plenty of support. Hands go up whenever a trainee has a question and a roving supervisor runs over to

57. https://www.amazon.com/When-Generations-Collide-Clash-Generational/dp/0066621070

58. https://www.saplinghr.com/blog/top-7-employee-onboarding-programs

help. Once on their own, employees work within teams. But they're never far from a helping hand as team leaders and "floor walkers" decked in bright vests of red or yellow are always available to answer questions.[59]

6. GAMIFICATION

Who says learning your new role can't be fun? Smart companies leverage play and gamification as part of their onboarding. Featured in the book *Work with Me*, **JP Morgan** invites candidates to play Fantasy Futures, an online trading game that's akin to Fantasy Football, to help candidates learn the business.[60]

Generation X desires to mix their fun with their work. Featured in *Ties to Tattoos*, Sherri Elliott shared the story of **WinStar World Casinos**.[61] When they needed to hire 1,100 employees for their gaming, hotel, and retail operations in the Midwest, they printed employment and benefit information on the back of playing cards. The cards featured WinStar's slogan: "At WinStar Casinos having fun is just part of the job." The campaign also included messaging that appealed specifically to Gen X's self-reliant and pragmatic nature. WinStar tailors specific recruiting messaging to Matures and Boomers as well. For those generations, they use messaging that highlights benefits, security, money, and that gaming is a growth industry.

7. CHECKING IN

When employees join **Davies PR**, they are given a 3-month, 6-month, 9-month, and a one-year review to ensure they get a

59. https://www.tampabay.com/news/business/workinglife/
    capital-ones-open-culture-helps-make-it-one-of-tampa-bays-top-workplaces/1227026
60. https://www.amazon.com/Work-Me-Leading-Multigenerational-Workforce-ebook/dp/B001LRPNJE
61. https://www.amazon.com/Ties-Tattoos-Generational-Differences-Competitive-ebook/dp/B004X34M40

"Best Start" at Davies. After the first year at the company, employees receive annual 360-degree reviews in which they are assessed by their co-workers.

Companies are using new tools and procedures to assimilate their latest hires. **Veson Nautical**, a Boston-based software developer for risk management for the maritime industry, instituted a new program called FastStart, an online tool from consulting firm Blessing White that aligns work styles and priorities between new employees and managers. "The manager ranks the skills important and less important to the job, and the employee does the same," says Sarah Taffee, Director of Human Resources and Organization Effectiveness at Veson Nautical. "The employee has the opportunity to compare their own answers with their manager's answers, and then the system guides them through how to have an open discussion about those things."[62]

Cardiff encourages employees to visit all the departments in the company during orientation and throughout their tenure. They've dispensed with the old belief that employees stick with a single function during their entire career. According to Lynne Lancaster and David Stillman in *When Generations Collide*, "They encourage employees to look around the company to see the next place they'd like to work. As a result, the next place is usually Cardiff and not a competitor."[63]

Lancaster and Stillman also share the example of **Galactic.**[64] The firm not only encourages employees to seek out other opportunities, but it supports career pathing even if it means with a different company. Galactic has a policy that if an employee would like to interview with another company, they get two days off, no questions asked. If they come back and put in their resignation, the company

62. https://www.inc.com/winning-workplaces/articles/201105/employee-onboarding-done-better.html
63. https://www.amazon.com/When-Generations-Collide-Clash-Generational/dp/0066621070
64. https://www.amazon.com/When-Generations-Collide-Clash-Generational/dp/0066621070

throws them a going-away party. If they come back and want to stay, then they are welcomed back with open arms. Galactic engenders goodwill by supporting Millennials in pursuing the career paths that are best for them, even if its not the best for the company.

RECRUITING AND ONBOARDING TAKEAWAY

Smart companies take advantage of these early days of recruiting and onboarding in order to ensure a strong, productive, and dedicated workforce.

Now, let's look at Vision and Purpose ...

CHAPTER 12

VISION AND PURPOSE

"The purpose of life is not to be happy. It is to be useful,
to be honorable, to be compassionate, to have it make
some difference that you have lived and lived well."

– Ralph Waldo Emerson

Vision and purpose are critical elements of employee engagement. Shane Green in his book *Culture Hacker* wrote that more than 50 percent of employees leave within the first year of their roles because they don't see their company's stated purpose lived out in the workplace. Leaders can say they have a stated purpose, but if employees don't see it, they walk. In particular, younger generations are more apt to question leadership and vote with their feet if they see something that seem disingenuous. Deloitte's 2017 Millennial study validates Green saying Millennials (as customers and employees) seek companies whose actions and behaviors display values congruent with their own.[65]

Let's look at 12 companies who are embracing purpose and bringing it to life across the generations.

8. STANDING UP BY CLOSING DOWN

REI embraces purpose. In 2015, they generated 6.7MM media impressions with their #OptOutside campaign, closing all their stores on Black Friday to encourage people to get outside. REI could have made money on Black Friday, but instead chose to support their ideals of outside activity. As a result, REI saw a 100 percent increase in applications for jobs receiving thousands of applications to fill 1,200 positions. Their employee retention is twice that of their retail competitors, and they have been listed on *Fortune's* Top 100 places to work for 19 years.[66]

9. FINDING A DEEPER PURPOSE

Cactus Feeders is the largest independently owned cattle feeding company in the world. The employee-owned company cares for

---

65. https://www2.deloitte.com/content/dam/Deloitte/global/Documents/About-Deloitte/gx-deloitte-millennial-survey-2017-executive-summary.pdf

66. https://newsroom.rei.com/company-information/statements/working-at-rei.htm

over one million animals a year. The company realized that for Millennials, a job in production agriculture is not one that's brag-worthy. In order to stand out, the company changed things to be a better fit for the younger X and Millennial generations. They wanted to go beyond dollars as they understood money wasn't the ultimate motivator. The board started exploring their purpose. Research told them that the world would be twice as hungry in 20 years, and it would need protein. They declared their purpose was to feed a hungry world. According the Haydn Shaw in the book *Sticking Points*, "Managers were willing to talk about it and the employees embraced it. All the generations rallied around this common purpose."[67]

The **Lung Transplant Foundation** works to embrace all the generations with their common purpose. Emily Everett, Executive Director, Lung Transplant Foundation shares:

> We focus on building depth and breadth across the organization as we work towards a common goal. Since lung diseases have no age-related boundaries, neither do we. While the Baby Boomers bring an array of experiences that have helped define and structure the organization, the inclusion of Millennials and Gen X team members add vibrancy and innovation that helps ensure our growth. As we share ideas, we look for compromises that bring sound, sustainable business practices.

Clarity of purpose helps give employees' work meaning—something particularly important to younger generations, but significant to Baby Boomers as well. Companies see purpose as the glue that unites a team and enables everyone to look beyond their individual tasks. In the words of Jeanne Bliss in *Would You Do That To Your*

---

67. https://www.amazon.com/Sticking-Points-Generations-Working-Together/dp/1414364717

Mother, "If the company has a clear view, they also link it to who they hire and what they'll do (and won't do) to grow.

For instance, **Gerber** is a trusted partner of parents and hasn't moved from that in 90 years. **IKEA** is about creating inexpensive furniture and a better everyday life for people. **Zappos** is all about service, and **DaVita** (a leading kidney-care company) has the purpose of "giving life."[68]

Millennials and Gen Z are very much driven by finding meaning in their work. But how can an organization help them find that meaning? "Purpose has become more true today than ever before," Shravanti Chakraborty, head of people at **Coursera**, told HR Dive in an email.[69] "We've been seeing for the last several years at places like Google and Coursera business is trying to understand what motivates people and makes the best teams. Meaning and purpose came out over and over in surveys." She feels this revolves around working to be more intentional. Chakraborty says the question is: "How do we think about purpose in one's work life and pull on that thread to engage employees ongoing—is it with managers or leaders or employees directly?"

Making an exercise on purpose. HR Dive also shares the story of **GreatCall**. "We begin each year with the opportunity to attend a creativity-based session where each employee chooses a word that will define their year," says Lynn Herrick, CHRO at GreatCall. "It's called 'One Little Word' and once an employee has selected their word, they define it, set small, attainable goals related to the word and create a piece of art that will inspire and remind them of that purpose throughout the year." Herrick started the activity specifically with the HR team about five years ago, and it was so popular that the team asked Herrick to implement it company-wide. "It has

68. https://www.amazon.com/Would-You-That-Your-Mother/dp/0735217815
69. https://www.hrdive.com/news/how-teaching-employees-to-find-their-purpose-can-lead-to-better-engagement/528325/

a profound effect on people and it's a great exercise for self-reflection and intention-setting."

10. PURPOSE FROM THE TOP DOWN

For employee development to truly take off, employee engagement needs to be embraced from the top down. Leaders need to create a deep sense of connectedness and pride tied to the broader purpose of the organization. According to Meredith Ferguson of **DoSomething Strategic**, "then create a spectrum of employee engagements that fosters leadership, trust, and purpose among your young employees. That's how you'll get them to stay, grow, and mentor others. That's how you move them from employees to true brand ambassadors."[70]

11. BELONGING AND FEELING VALUED

Warmth is critical in business. Having a sense of belonging and feeling part of something bigger than yourself is critical for engagement. Melanie Frost, Major, **U.S. Air Force Reserve** shared with us how this plays out in military life:

> Many of us have had a fantasy about slipping off anonymously to lay around on a beach the rest of our lives. Counterintuitively, this course of action may not be the best for our psychological health. A spate of recent studies [has] shown that humans thrive when two conditions are met: 1. we must feel a sense of belonging and 2. believe that our labor is important. We often look to our workplace to fulfill these two fundamental human needs, though some are better organized to provide our place and purpose. The

---

70. https://www.hrdive.com/news/how-teaching-employees-to-find-their-purpose-can-lead-to-better-engagement/528325/

military is exceptional at giving its members a sense of belonging and importance. Each service abounds in ways that make a member feel part of the "in-group." Everyone must complete rites of passage such as basic training, technical schools, and fitness tests. Service-specific jargon typified in TLAs (three letter acronyms) create a common language. If you understand me when I say, "As a CGO, I went on an OCONUS TDY where the DFAC only served MREs," you have probably been in the military. For those of you who haven't, this translates to "as a young officer, I went on an overseas business trip where the cafeteria only served prepackaged meals." Uniforms, rank, ribbons/medals, and unit patches instantly identify someone not only as a military member, but which subgroups that individual belongs in. Units also have legends, songs, traditions, heroes, symbols, mascots and mottoes which the civilian world may only experience at school or with sports teams.

Taken altogether, many servicemembers understand that they may take a bullet for a coworker and assume those around them would do the same for them. This sense of belonging fosters the trust necessary for life-and-death assignments. In fact, communicating the high stakes to servicemembers is the cornerstone of how the military makes its individuals feel their effort is important. Everyone from the general commanding operations in active conflicts to the troop turning wrenches in Kansas is told that his or her efforts protect the lives of their families and fellow servicemembers and the very foundation of the free world. It is telling that the Soldier's Creed includes "I am a guardian of freedom and the American way of life." Military members are constantly feted in codified quarterly awards programs, promotions, and with ribbons and medals. Annual performance reports are less critical feedback and more a highlight reel of accomplishments told in action-impact-results form. Supervisors take great pains to link each individual's actions to missions and lives saved. Is it any wonder, then, that many veterans have a crisis of identity when leaving the service? A common refrain from veterans, especially those forced to leave due to injury, is that they miss the sense of camaraderie and purpose they had while in the military. I have learned a lot from my military service on how to foster community and communicate worth to coworkers and family members. While a "full court press" of military attributes would be disingenuous for many organizations, small tweaks can make a big difference. Instead of treating a work-intensive quarterly budget report as a pain to get through, treat it as a rite of passage with extra recognition and privileges on the other side. When thanking a team member, be sure to mention not just the difficulty of the task but how completing the task made an impact to the organization or customers. Most importantly, though many people would like a short-term reprieve from responsibilities, no one wants to feel lonely or useless. Our psychological health depends on knowing how we fit in and [on] completing difficult tasks that are considered important to others.

12. THE SAME PAGE AND THE RIGHT FOOT

Mike Wittenstein, President and CEO of StoryMiners, shares this story about **Big Peach Running Company**. Their purpose is to help runners find their correct shoe fit.

Big Peach, a specialty footwear and gear store based in Atlanta, has a secret to their success as the go-to store for people serious about their outdoor activity. First, store associates fit your foot. They don't ask about style or brand or budget, they get to know your feet, your running/walking style (some pretty cool camera- and sensor-equipment machines help them), and your objectives. Once [they] find the right fit, everyone knows what size/shape/performance your shoes need to be. Then, the shopping begins. With everyone on the same page about feet first, it's much easier to then find the best pair(s) of shoes. Camaraderie is high between employees and engagement is high between customers. Teens to seniors fit into this model and everyone learns from everyone else. The returns policy is liberal so that customers feel secure in their purchases, especially when trying new brands. Employees aren't penalized for returns. Big Peach shows up at all the local meets in a show of support. It's not uncommon for the person who helped you find shoes in the store to hand you a water bottle on a run.

VISION AND PURPOSE TAKEAWAY

Leaders need to be authentic. You can never fake your way through leadership—especially with younger, more critical generations. A strong vision and purpose is key for engagement.

Now, let's look at Training and Development ...

CHAPTER 13

TRAINING AND DEVELOPMENT

"Job training empowers people to realize their dreams and improve their lives."

– Sylvia Mathews Burwell

Investing in your employees involves training and development. You need to invest the time and resources to position team members for success. A great example of this is **Wegmans**. The New York based supermarket invests in training for store openings. They seek to promote from within and then train the new teams for 14 weeks to get everyone ready to act. According to Jeanne Bliss in *Would You Do That To Your Mother*, "They won't expand until the right people are ready, available and in place to deliver the right experience. Half of the store managers started working as teenagers and they consider their green apron a badge of honor. Turnover is just four percent for full-time employees and they've been ranked in the Top 100 companies to work for over 20 consecutive years."[71]

Let's look at 12 more companies that go the extra mile to allow employees to learn how to become the best version of themselves.

13. EXPERIENTIAL LEARNING

Younger generations learned from Sesame Street and other programs that made learning fun. Because of that, old methods that worked for Matures and Boomers don't work now. **UPS** saw firsthand the time to train their drivers go from 30 to 90 (and sometimes 180) days. To remedy that, they added hands-on experiential learning. For example, they filmed trainees lifting packages so they could see what they're doing right and wrong. According to the book *Work With Me*, "[UPS used] a transparent package car to show where and how to place packages."[72]

When Boomers tried to use PowerPoint to pass on experiences to Millennials, the younger generation said they learn better with

---

71. https://www.amazon.com/Would-You-That-Your-Mother/dp/0735217815

72. https://www.amazon.com/Work-Me-Leading-Multigenerational-Workforce-ebook/dp/B001LRPNJE

interactive methods. **Lockheed** now offers workshops for managers on generational diversity emphasizing the different learning styles.[73]

14. CONTINUING ED

Scripps learned about the desire of Baby Boomers to continue learning throughout their lifetime and offered employee opportunities that tap into personal beliefs and aspirations. The book *Generations at Work* shared the story of Bruce Grendell. The 20-year employee and Baby Boomer used Scripps' tuition reimbursement to earn his master's degree in nursing and advance his career.[74]

AT&T built an "always-on" learning model that encourages (and forces) everyone to develop themselves on a continuous basis.

15. GROWING LEADERS

Ameriprise created the Young Professionals Network (YPN) to help Millennials grow their leadership and working skills. In peer learning groups, the members meet regularly in small groups to help each other. As shared in *Generations at Work*, Ameriprise created two levels of generational education for all employees.[75] Level 1 helps employees understand how the different generations want to communicate. Level 2 dives deeper into ways leaders can leverage unique perspectives of different generations to increase business value.

73. https://www.amazon.com/Generations-Work-Managing-Boomers-Workplace/dp/0814432336

74. https://www.amazon.com/Generations-Work-Managing-Boomers-Workplace/dp/0814432336

75. https://www.amazon.com/Generations-Work-Managing-Boomers-Workplace/dp/0814432336

16. COMMUNICATING AND SUPPORTING

The **U.S. Air Force Academy** changed their training to create a more supportive environment for Millennials and Gen Z. For previous generations, lunch used to be a time for upper classmen to train freshmen by making them recite Air Force facts and procedures before the meal. The freshmen would then pass up all the table's food to the seniors to take their portions, then it was handed to the juniors and so on. If there was little food left, the freshmen ate less. Now, the freshmen eat first because "leaders eat last," and they are not required to train before the meal.

Randstad offers training for leaders on how to communicate with younger generations. It has reduced first-year turnover from 50 to 30 percent.

17. INDIVIDUALIZED LEARNING

In an effort to retain more Millennials, **Mobilize** creates a leadership development plan for every individual. According to *Generations at Work*, "They map a path from the role an employee currently has to the one they ultimately want (like CEO). They then discuss how you get there, what you need to do and where they want to see the employee grow."[76]

18. VIDEO AND MORE VIDEO

The single biggest thing that Millennials said organizations need to change to attract top talent was better employee development. Millennials are typically characterized as being entitled in what they request for themselves so early in their careers, but it is less of a generational personality trait than it is their basic experience growing up in the digital age.

---

76. https://www.amazon.com/Generations-Work-Managing-Boomers-Workplace/dp/0814432336

The **American Society for Surgery of the Hand** has a digital initiative called "Hand-e." It is an e-learning portal where the organization is working to place every single piece of digital content created by the Association. The portal contains thousands of hours of streaming video, as well as conference presentations and online courses for surgeons. According to Jamie Notter and Maddie Grant in the book *When Millennials Take Over*, "The content is available to ASSH members for free. There were already 500,000 pieces of unique content within one year of the site going live. The concept was conceived in a brainstorm."[77]

19. MAKE TRAINING A LAUGHING MATTER

About a decade ago, Steve Cody, one of Peppercomm's founders and a managing partner, started taking stand-up comedy classes for fun. He worked with Clayton Fletcher, a touring stand-up comedian, to build his chops. "As he started doing more and more stand-up, he started to recognize that although he was very good at client meetings and presentations, he was getting a lot better," says Deborah Brown, Partner and Managing Director, Strategic Development.[78] Brown credits the training with developing not only speaking skills but listening skills as well. It wasn't long before the entire management committee at **Peppercomm** was taking comedy training. It was sprung on the team at an offsite meeting. Soon after that, everyone in the company was involved. "For the past five years, it's become part of our DNA," Brown says. In fact, comedy training is now mandatory at the agency and is part of the onboarding process. The training consists of learning about different types of comedy such as observational humor. It's become a great way to meet the new hires with "graduation" consisting of a five-minute set of stand-up. The agency has created fundraisers out of the performances and has even incorporated them into agency

---

77. https://www.amazon.com/When-Millennials-Take-Over-Ridiculously/dp/1940858127

78. https://purplegoldfish.com/employee-engagement-is-a-laughing-matter-peppercom/

offsite meetings. The training has become an integral part of Peppercomm. Deborah Brown credits it with improving productivity, building teamwork, and injecting fun into the agency. Humor is now part of the fabric of Peppercomm, whether it takes the form of spicing up an interoffice email or creating a funny video for a client pitch.

20. TRAINING LEADERS

Chicago-based online advertising buyer **Centro** focuses on the manager-employee relationship. Centro spends a lot of time training managers. Why? Because people quit bosses, not jobs. The biggest reason employees leave is because of their managers. Scott Golas, Vice President of Human Resources, says his company focuses on the manager-employee relationship. He shared in an article in Crain's, "Let's face it: People leave companies because of their boss."[79]

21. EMOTIONAL INTELLIGENCE

Oberoi Group in India, manager of exclusive high-end properties, invests in emotional intelligence training for employees. According to Jeanne Bliss in *Would You Do That to Your Mother*, "Instead of having their frontline/customer-facing employees guided by a manual or set of rules, they invest in coaching training that leads to the right response for the right guest. Armed with this training, employees can build the skill set they need to react properly to situations."[80]

---

79. https://www.chicagobusiness.com/article/20120331/ISSUE02/120329728/
    chicago-s-best-places-to-work-2012-why-your-perks-aren-t-working
80. https://www.amazon.com/Would-You-That-Your-Mother/dp/0735217815

TRAINING AND DEVELOPMENT TAKEAWAY

It's not a one-size-fits-all proposition when it comes to training. The different generations learn in a variety of ways.

Now let's look at Flexing ...

CHAPTER 14

FLEXING

"I want to caution you against the idea that balance has to be a routine that looks the same week in and week out."

– Kevin Thoman

Flexing is about control, and every generation wants flexibility. According to the Center for Talent Innovation's research, if there's one work perk that rises above the rest across the generations, it's flexible work arrangements. The CTI study showed that 87 percent of Boomers, 79 percent of Gen Xers and 89 percent of Millennials cite flexibility as important.[81]

Why offer flexibility? The two main benefits are increased productivity and greater job satisfaction. According to Sylvia Ann Hewlett in *Harvard Business Review*:[82]

> Companies that treat time as currency—through remote work options, staggered hours, and reduced-hour arrangements—are also more likely to attract and retain high-caliber employees. Work/life balance has always been prized by working women juggling the demands of family and high-powered jobs, and now these moms are being seconded by incoming Millennials, who consider it a basic entitlement to play as hard as they work.

Here are statistics the 2018 Deloitte Millennial Study:[83]

> 43 percent of Millennials envision leaving their jobs within two years. Only 28 percent seek to stay beyond five years. The 15-point gap is up from seven points last year.
>
> Employed Generation Z respondents express even less loyalty, with 61 percent saying they would leave within two years if given the choice. For Generation

81. https://hbr.org/2012/05/attract-and-keep-a-players-wit
82. https://hbr.org/2012/05/attract-and-keep-a-players-wit
83. https://www2.deloitte.com/global/en/pages/about-deloitte/articles/millennialsurvey.html

Z, which has fewer financial obligations, monetary rewards placed second behind the desire to be part of a positive workplace culture.

Not only do Millennials appreciate not being tied to strict hours or locations, they also value the trust their employers demonstrate in granting that flexibility. Among those who intend to stay with their current employers for at least five years, 55 percent say there is now more flexibility in where and when they work compared to three years ago. Among those looking to leave within the next 24 months, the figure is only 35 percent.

Let's look at 10 companies that leverage flexibility to drive engagement.

22. ROWE YOUR BOAT

Best Buy created the "Results-Only Work Environment" (ROWE) that was so successful that it spun-off into a consulting business, Culture Rx. The philosophy tells people that they are free to do their work wherever and whenever they want—as long as they achieve the desired results. Employees report they have increased control over their schedules and that gives them more dignity, freedom, and the work/life balance they want. ROWE works best for work teams (rather than individuals) who go through the training together and experience new ways to work. There needs to be a team culture around the change so an individual is not singled out. In *Work with Me,* Debra Magnuson and Lora Alexander say, "There must also be a freedom to say "no" to noncritical meetings. In order for the system to work, employees need to know exactly what is expected of them with clearly defined outcomes/measurements, training, feedback and accountability."[84]

E&Y has 10 percent of their employees on flex work schedules and that group includes 100 employees who have received promotions while working flex schedules. E&Y has saved $10 million a year through improved retention.[85]

23. JOB SHARING AND FLEX SCHEDULES

SAS is a forward thinker when it comes to job sharing, flex schedules, and a 35-hour work week to accommodate activities outside work. Likewise, they have a variety of concierge amenities like on-site dry cleaning and day care.

USAA is also known for having onsite amenities.

24. IT'S NOT A ONE-SIZE-FITS-ALL SCENARIO

Deloitte managers were complaining that employees now weren't willing to work weekends as other generations had. Their HR department created a generational brochure to educate managers on how to adapt to employees' preferred schedules and to generational differences in general. The brochure is widely used by managers.[86]

An angry 49 percent of employees think meetings are a waste of time. Haydn featured **Memorial Hermann-Texas Medical Center** in his book *Sticking Points.*[87] The medical center has figured out a number of different ways to keep generations engaged in meetings. They cut down relationship building time (that was important to Boomers) to shorten the meetings (appreciated by Xers and

---

84. https://www.amazon.com/Work-Me-Leading-Multigenerational-Workforce-ebook/dp/B001LRPNJE
85. https://www.amazon.com/Generations-Work-Managing-Boomers-Workplace/dp/0814432336
86. https://www.amazon.com/Generations-Work-Managing-Boomers-Workplace/dp/0814432336
87. https://www.amazon.com/Sticking-Points-Generations-Working-Together/dp/1414364717

Millennials). Head of Nursing Victoria King started texting Gen X directors for input electronically before meetings, eliminating the need for feedback around the table. Xers agreed to put away their iPads (this had annoyed Boomers).

25. FLEXING FOR FAMILY

Former **Google** Executive Marissa Mayer believes women are especially susceptible to burning out because they are faced with more demands in the home. "What causes burnout, Mayer believes, is not working too hard," Hanna Rosin writes in her *Business Insider* interview with Mayer.[88] People, she [Mayer] believes, "can work arbitrarily hard for an arbitrary amount of time," but they will become resentful if work makes them miss things that are really important to them. Mayer gave an anecdote for how she kept one Google executive, whom she calls "Katy" from quitting.

Katy loved her job and she loved her team and she didn't mind staying late to help out. What was bothering Katy was something entirely different. Often, Katy confessed, she showed up late at her children's events because a meeting went overly long for no important reason other than meetings tend to go long. And she hated having her children watch her walk in late. For Mayer, this was a no-brainer. She instituted a Katy-tailored rule. If Katy had told her earlier that she had to leave at four to get to a soccer game, then Mayer would make sure Katy could leave at four. Even if there was only five minutes left to a meeting, even if Google co-founder Sergey Brin himself was mid-sentence and expecting an answer from Katy, Mayer would say, 'Katy's gotta go,' and Katy would walk out the door and answer the questions later by e-mail after the kids were in bed.

---

88. https://www.businessinsider.com/marissa-mayer-tip-on-preventing-employee-burn-out-2012-9

26. SCHEDULE FLEXIBILITY

Work schedule flexibility is a major reason why employees prefer working at **Busch Gardens**. It has helped make the Tampa Bay theme park a go-to employer. According to David Bode, VP of Human Resources in a *Tampa Bay Tribune* article,[89] "We learned how to be very flexible because we employ a lot of students with strange hours and people who rely on us for second jobs. Plus, our work demand varies so much." Busch needs a minimum of 1,500 people to keep the park open seven days a week. They bulk the staff up to 4,500 for the peak summer and winter seasons between Christmas and Easter. But needs vary dramatically with weather, the day of the week, the time of day, and attendance projections, so the park has made schedule juggling an art form. "It's great," said Chris Noyce, a 21-year-old USF environmental sciences major in his third year as a ride operator. "When you work is almost up to you." Employees post their availability on a company website. Shifts are pared down to work units of four to six hours. The computer matches available employees to attendance projections and work demands two weeks ahead of time. The supervisors then fine-tune and juggle the actual work assignments, even down to the same day.

27. RETHINKING VACATION

Believe it or not, **Point B**, a Portland management consulting company, offers its employees no paid vacation time or holidays and the employees seem to love it. That's because this company believes so firmly in flexibility that associates get paid only for the time they work, so there is no arbitrary limit to how much time off they can take. "I've never worked anywhere that was as committed to helping

---

89. http://www.tampabay.com/news/business/workinglife/
   work-schedule-flexibility-is-a-major-attraction-at-busch-gardens/1226658

employees realize what the work-life balance means to them individually" shared one employee to *Oregon Business.*[90]

28. FLEXING MOMS

Lifetime National School Studios, the company that takes all those millions of school portraits, has relied on Boomer and Xer moms to staff their part-time photographer positions. Shared by Lynne Lancaster and David Stillman in *When Generations Collide,* "The work occurred during school hours, was usually close to home, and involved being with kids—a perfect match for moms looking to supplement family income without taking much time away from the home front."[91]

FLEXING TAKEAWAY

The key to sustaining (earning and maintaining) loyalty from employees across the generations is making sure they get to do the things that are most important to them outside of work.

Now, let's look at Project Management ...

90. http://www.oregonbusiness.com/articles/112-march-2012/6795-the-2012-list-top-33-small-companies-to-work-for-in-oregon?start=3

91. https://www.amazon.com/When-Generations-Collide-Clash-Generational/dp/0066621070

CHAPTER 15

PROJECT MANAGEMENT

"Operations keeps the lights on, strategy provides a light at the end of the tunnel, but project management is the train engine that moves the organization forward."

– Joy Gumz

Command and Control or Carrot and Stick thinking is outdated. People do not enjoy or appreciate being controlled or coerced. According to **Netflix**, "The best managers figure out how to get great outcomes by setting the appropriate context rather than by trying to control their people."[92] Leaders have to become adept at project management across the generations. "We are finding that giving people a chance to succeed in their job and setting them free to a certain degree is the key to motivation, as opposed to trying to direct and control people's energy. It's really about letting go and connecting people to their work, and each other, rather than channeling, organizing, orchestrating, and focusing behavior," says Ken Blanchard.[93]

Let's look at 10 companies and how they handle project management.

29. TRANSPARENCY AND OPENNESS MATTERS

Vineet Nayar, former CEO of **HCL Technologies,** touched on transparency in his bestselling book, *Employees First, Customers Second.*[94] In the book, Nayar outlined four ways that transparency builds trust:

> Transparency ensures that every stakeholder knows the company vision and understands how their contribution assists the organization in achieving its goals. Working in an environment without transparency is like trying to solve a jigsaw puzzle without knowing what the finished picture is supposed to look like.
>
> It ensures that every stakeholder has a deep personal commitment to the aims of the organization.

---

92. https://www.slideshare.net/reed2001/culture-2009/2-Reference_Guide_on_ourFreedom_ResponsibilityCultureThese
93. https://www.fastcompany.com/3002382/why-trying-manipulate-employee-motivation-always-backfires
94. https://www.amazon.com/Employees-First-Customers-Second-Conventional/dp/1422139069

Gen Y members expect transparency as a given. They post their life stories in public domains; they expect nothing less in their workplaces.

In a knowledge economy, we want customers to be transparent with us, to share their ideas, their vision and their strategies for solving core problems. Why would customers be transparent with us if we don't trust employees enough to be transparent with them?

To proactively promote openness, HCL put together an online forum for employees called U&I. Employees could ask any question to the senior team at HCL Technologies. It was an open site where everyone could see the question, the questioner, and the answer. Employees responded favorably as noted by this comment: "This is the biggest change we have seen at HCL in years. Now we have a management team that is willing to acknowledge the dirt."

Why open the window of information? Vineet uses the analogy of an Amsterdam window. Having previously lived on the Herengracht ("Gentleman's Canal") in Amsterdam, Stan can attest that these windows are immense. They are a throwback to the modest Calvinist period when subtle expressions of wealth, such as being able to afford to pay the highest window tax, were favored by the rich. In the words of writer Joanna Tweedy, "Today, the centuries-old glass, beautifully imperfect, frames the olive-green waters outside and lets the natural light, and the eyes of curious tourists, pour in." While visiting Amsterdam, Vineet pointed to windows and asked his friend, "Why so large?" The friend mentioned all the obvious reasons like letting in light and enjoying the view of the canal, but then offered a much more interesting answer. He shared, "It keeps the house clean." It turns out that the bigger your windows, the more glass you have, the more visible your dirt will be, to you and to everyone who visits or passes by. In Vineet's words, If you can see the dirt, you will be much more likely to get rid of it. A transparent house has a dramatic effect on the culture inside.[95]

Before the merger with Amazon, **Whole Foods** tried to be as transparent with their employees as possible. CEO John Mackey believes a "culture of shared information helps create a culture of 'shared fate' among employees." They made a practice of sharing employee's salaries, daily store sales data, and weekly regional sales data. In the book *When Millennials Take Over*, Jaime Notter and Maddie Grant share that, "[Whole Foods] does this not to be provocative, but to enable individuals and teams at their stores throughout the country to make better decisions. Bonuses are team based, so if you achieve certain metrics (say for the Produce department), you trigger a bonus for your whole team. The result is a system that is agile and can make quick changes based on market conditions."[96]

30. EMPOWERING EMPLOYEES

In *Turn the Ship Around*, Navy Captain David Marquet shares how he turned his submarine from one of the worst in the **U.S Navy** to the best by empowering his leaders.[97] Often times, leaders are afraid to empower because they fear they'll lose control or because of a lack of trust in their subordinates. Marquet created the right culture and was successful.

Vail Resorts doesn't want their frontline people following scripts. Instead, they want them to bend any rule they need to in order to deliver customer joy. This is reinforced by "joy reinforcement" where coaching and reviews focus on the behaviors employees exhibit to make fun happen. The resort empowers employees to be inclusive, welcoming, approachable, and positive. Vail has earned

---

95. https://www.amazon.com/Employees-First-Customers-Second-Conventional/dp/1422139069

96. https://www.amazon.com/When-Millennials-Take-Over-Ridiculously/dp/1940858127

97. https://www.amazon.com/Turn-Ship-Around-Turning-Followers/dp/1591846404

Best Overall Customer Service Program three times according to Jeanne Bliss in *Would You Do That to Your Mother.*[98] Their employees cite the ability to "deliver the experience of a lifetime" as the main driver in working there.

Bliss also cites **Alaska Airlines** and **Safelite**. Alaska Airlines has earned the JD Power award for highest customer satisfaction 10 years in a row. One of the ways they do it is by letting their employees do what they think is right. Their COO says, "We trust you. You'll never get in trouble for making a decision and we don't want you to call the supervisor." Gen X loves this and so do customers. Give me a vision and get out of my way!

Safelite encourages and trusts employees to make decisions based on what they perceive to be the right decision. The company wants employees to feel comfortable living in the "gray." They can decide when to make exceptions. CEO Tom Feeney says he's seen a big change in the behavior of his front line and how they personalize the work they do to accommodate different customers.

Morning Star is a tomato processing company with factories, trucks, and farms. It has no managers and every single employee, including seasonal workers, has the authority to purchase whatever equipment he or she needs to get the job done. This is a $700 million-per-year business with as many as 2,400 employees during peak season. According to Jamie Notter and Maddie Grant in *When Millennials Take Over*, "Not a single one of those employees at Morning Star needs approval to make a purchase."[99]

---

98. https://www.amazon.com/Would-You-That-Your-Mother/dp/0735217815
99. https://www.amazon.com/When-Millennials-Take-Over-Ridiculously/dp/1940858127Ocv

31. BENEFITS OF A SHARED VISION FOR PROJECT MANAGEMENT

PatchPlus Consulting's strong shared vision to continue to make a difference helps with balancing the three generations of its work force. PatchPlus is a small company with just over 50 employees scattered among 20 states and while it may seem like a homogenous group of former Air Force intelligence specialists, there is a span of generations (84% Gen Xers, 10% Millennials, 6% Baby Boomers). The PatchPlus business model is a collaborative think-tank teaming approach and offers customers flexible support for a specific task or a broad range of projects. This model allows for PatchPlus personnel to contribute their strengths to different projects. Most efforts are done remotely with little administrative overhead and the best match of experience for the project is tasked. The caliber of employees is superb. All are highly trained subject matter experts who are self-motivated and proactive. According to Beth Kwasny, Director, ISR Technical Support, PatchPlus Consulting, "Creating a professional team with a shared vision overcomes the generational differences to contribute to the success of PatchPlus."

A shared vision can also work in professional services. Traditionally in law firms, work is distributed by layers. A senior partner generates work and hands it off to a junior partner, who filters a project to a mid-level associate, who then might filter it down to an entry-level attorney. The problem with this top-down approach is that it can make it very difficult for those on the bottom of the totem pole to understand their role in the bigger picture. According to Lynne Lancaster and David Stillman in *When Generations Collide*, the law firm **Alston & Bird** does a good job of eliminating the unnecessary layers:

> Junior lawyers work directly with senior lawyers and gain valuable experience. As one attorney puts it, 'I see the nature of the whole project and not a narrow

perspective or snapshot. I truly understand how my work fits in … whether it's a large or small transaction. This really allows me to feel I am making a difference.' Lawyers at the firm use the word 'own' a lot. The senior lawyers encourage the newer lawyers to own their work. By eliminating the unnecessary filtering and [by] fostering camaraderie among all generations of attorneys, a natural form of mentoring takes place.[100]

32. CHECKING-IN

U.S. Air Force Academy (and other service academy) applications are especially rigorous with multiple levels of the application that include a physical fitness evaluation and a medical exam beyond the normal transcripts and essays. They also include an interview with an Admissions Officer. In addition, Academy applicants must also apply for a nomination from their Congressional representatives (Congressperson or Senator). The process is similar to applying to another college with transcripts, essays, and often times an interview. Because Millennial and Gen Z applicants have had so much support from their parents with other school projects throughout their lives, Academy admissions officers have learned that they need to be more involved in their candidates' application packages. This means more reminders, more check ins, and more coaching to ensure the applicants complete their applications.

PROJECT MANAGEMENT TAKEAWAY

Empower your employees and understand how each generation needs to be managed.

Let's now look at recognition and motivation …

---

100. https://www.amazon.com/When-Generations-Collide-Clash-Generational/dp/0066621070

CHAPTER 16

RECOGNITION AND MOTIVATION

"Be lavish in your praise and hearty in your approbation. A drop of honey gathers more bees than a gallon of gall [vinegar]."

– Dale Carnegie

Reaching the heart of your employees across the generations involves recognition. According to Angela Maiers, "YOU MATTER. These two words can change your mood, change your mind, and have the power to change lives and the world if we understand and leverage them in the right way." Recognition resonates in the workplace. Thanking people for their hard work and commitment is key to making them feel appreciated at work.

Recognition fuels a sense of worth and belonging in individuals. No rocket science here, as humans we crave acceptance. Most managers take an "if, then" approach to recognition. Shawn Achor believes this paradigm needs to change "from thinking that encouragement and recognition should be used as rewards for high performance ... to thinking that encouragement and recognition are drivers of high performance."[101]

Let's look at seven companies and how they handle recognition.

33. POWER OF THE PEN

Former CEO of the **Campbell Soup Company** Doug Conant is a big proponent of the power of handwritten notes. Here are Doug's words in a *Harvard Business Review* article,

> Look for opportunities to celebrate. My executive assistants and I would spend a good 30 to 60 minutes a day scanning my mail and our internal website looking for news of people who have made a difference at Campbell's. Get out your pen. Believe it or not, I have sent roughly 30,000 handwritten notes to employees over the last decade, from maintenance people to senior executives. I let them know that I am personally

---

101. http://goodthinkinc.com/about/

paying attention and celebrating their accomplishments. (I send handwritten notes too because well over half of our associates don't use a computer.) I also jump on any opportunities to write to people who partner with our company any time I meet with them. It's the least you can do for people who do things to help your company and industry. On the face of it, writing handwritten notes may seem like a waste of time. But in my experience, they build goodwill and lead to higher productivity.[102]

Indra Nooyi, former CEO of **Pepsi**, personally writes letters to the parents of her top 400 executives. According to Jeanne Bliss in *Would You Do That to Your Mother,* she thanks them for instilling the values in them that are directly benefiting Pepsi. Nooyi writes, "Thank you for the gift of your child to our company."[103]

34. ALLOWING EMPLOYEES TO FIND THE RIGHT BALANCE

Companies that are the most flexible about helping employees achieve some level of balance seem to have an easier time recruiting, managing, and retaining employees. These companies typically have lower turnover, a less stressed workforce, lower absenteeism, and better morale. Balance doesn't have to cost a fortune. Sometimes all it takes is showing a little support for employees' avocations. Featured in the book *When Generations Collide*, **Bridge Works** has funded a kayak class, tickets to the Westminster Kennel Club Dog Show, and paid for an employee to join a fitness center. None applies to the work they do, but all help the work get done. Larry Perlman shares:

---

102. http://blogs.hbr.org/cs/2011/02/secrets_of_positive_feedback.html

103. https://www.amazon.com/Would-You-That-Your-Mother/dp/0735217815

What was always the right thing to do has become the smart thing to do. A one-size-fits-all generations approach to rewards just won't work. That said, carte blanche doesn't work either. Rewards should be tailored to the generations. Tailor rewards that fit the life stages of employees in ways that have meaning to them. One of the rewards a-la-carte at Bridge Works for an employee was coming in late three days a week in order to drive his daughter to nursery school. Does it disrupt things? Not really. The employee just rearranges his workload and every so often they cover his calls. Cost to Bridge Work ... nothing. The employee getting to stop for doughnuts and have some one-on-one with his daughter ... priceless.[104]

35. CELEBRATING DAILY

Many Millennials and Generation Z children were raised with star charts. When they did something good, they were rewarded by having a star placed next to their name on the refrigerator. Likewise, they received nearly instantaneous feedback from friends when they posted something online. When these generations entered the workforce, they were frustrated by the lack of feedback from their managers. Many companies provide mandatory feedback annually and some never do it at all. That's a tough transition when you're used to getting feedback on a daily basis. **Zuora**, a subscription management company, uses technology tools and forums that recognize and celebrate employee achievements as they occur, not a year later. They've found that this promotes individual growth across the generations, not just with Millennials. It also makes it easier for Generation X managers—people who oftentimes like to

---

work independently and have a hands-off approach to management—to provide real-time feedback.[105]

Millennials have been receiving their recognition high on social media for years now, so companies employing this generation will really have to step up their game. **Flackable** has figured out a way to attract and retain its Millennial workers. On day one of the job, the new hires get welcomed to the team with a new-hire press release. After the first day jitters are over, employees are encouraged to contribute to blog posts, articles, and more, so they can continually have a way to receive that recognition they love.[106]

36. RENEWING EMPLOYEES

Organizations must consider the "renewal factor" in understanding how to keep that person motivated and turned on. It may be something as simple as allowing a little longer vacation or the use of a corporate apartment in another city. Or it might mean arranging for a few months off to welcome a new child or pursue a passion. In *When Generations Collide*, Lynne Lancaster and David Stillman share how **Charles Schwab** let one of their contract employees take three-months off to focus on his first love—composing music. Because his work is critical to his department, his managers at Schwab are prepared to welcome him back into the fold when his three months of renewal are up.[107]

37. RECOGNIZING THE SANDWICH EFFECT

Xers and Boomers face the sandwich effect. This is pressure put on them by having aging parents and growing children at the very

105. https://medium.com/@tientzuo/3-ways-this-gen-x-ceo-tries-to-attract-millennial-talent-with-a-response-from-the-millennial-60d2eb9c43ad
106. https://www.inc.com/brian-hart/how-promoting-your-company-can-help-you-attract-retain-top-millennial-talent.html
107. https://www.amazon.com/When-Generations-Collide-Clash-Generational/dp/0066621070

same time they are at the apex of their career achievements and earning power. Given these constraints, time may be more valuable than money when thinking about rewards. Employees at **SC Johnson** are rewarded with access to an errand-running service.[108]

RECOGNITION AND MOTIVATION TAKEAWAY

You can't recognize employees too often. It's important to understand the different types of awards that appeal to each generation. Make a point to recognize regularly, promptly, and meaningfully.

Let's now have a look at Feedback and Mentoring ...

---

108. https://www.amazon.com/When-Generations-Collide-Clash-Generational/dp/0066621070

CHAPTER 17

FEEDBACK AND MENTORING

*"People won't stay and won't succeed
if they feel like outsiders and if they feel unsupported."*

– Spencer Rascoff

L et's face it—people do leave companies because of their manager. A shocking 70 percent of employees who voluntarily leave don't quit their jobs. They quit their boss. Former **Centro** SVP Scott Golas says, "We try to remove the typical obstacles (between bosses and employees) by sharing more information, by providing great training and by making sure those bosses have the right skill sets." Those skills involve feedback and mentoring.

Want to increase employee engagement? It's not brain surgery. The single biggest driver is the quality of the relationship with the employee's direct manager. Companies need to place an emphasis on developing managers of people across the generations. There are great benefits for getting it right. Gallup interviewed 10 million employees around the world. They asked them the following question: "Would you agree with this statement: 'My supervisor or somebody at work cares about me as a person?'"

Those who agreed

- were more productive.

- made greater contributions to profits.

- were more likely to stay with the company long term.

Let's look at 10 companies that leverage feedback and mentoring to drive engagement.

38. MIXED-AGE TEAMS

The challenges of managing a multigenerational workforce are on full display at **Pitney Bowes**. There, Brigitte Van Den Houte, Vice President of Human Resources and Global Talent Management, must persuade employees in their twenties that they have a future at the Stamford, Connecticut, based company, especially as it makes a push into e-commerce services to offset falling demand for its traditional postage-meter equipment. According to an article in the *Wall Street Journal*, at the same time, she must also encourage veterans 50 and older who make up about one-third of the workforce to support and even take direction from the newcomers.[109] Every few months Van Den Houte invites a group of young employees to spend a day with seasoned executives who share their knowledge about the company history and operations and offer advice about how to get ahead. And to spur growth in the e-commerce business, she has helped create mixed-age teams of about 15 employees from different departments with IT, sales, legal, and other experience. Decisions are made collaboratively and young employees have as much say as long-tenured ones. "The old way of working with employees more segregated by age and skills and veterans typically having the most authority no longer works," says Van Den Houte.

39. CREATE AN ENVIRONMENT OF SHARING

Challenge: How do you get older workers, often fearful of losing their jobs, to help younger employees? Vanessa Contreras, Vice President of Human Resources and Manufacturing at **McRoskey Mattress Co.** in San Francisco, says that when she joined the 119-year-old maker of handcrafted mattresses and box springs a decade ago, 90 percent of the company's nearly three-dozen employees were over 50. To woo young workers needed for the future, Contreras promised to train them to do several jobs so they could advance. But she first had to assure veterans that they wouldn't lose their jobs if they shared their knowledge. She told them the company wasn't planning to cut staff, as it had during the financial crisis, and she reminded them that they have seniority protection through their union. Eventually a few old-timers retired, allowing some

---

109. https://www.wsj.com/articles/the-tricky-task-of-managing-the-new-multigenerational-workplace-1534126021

young employees who had mastered multiple skills to advance to senior production jobs.

40. TWO-WAY MENTORING

Reverse or reciprocal mentoring programs, which pair young and seasoned talent, also promote knowledge sharing across generations. **Bon Secours Virginia Health System** of Richmond, Virginia, has formal and informal mentoring programs for its 14,000 employees, one-third of whom are over 50 and who range in age from 18 to 93. Among these is a program that each year identifies about 75 high-potential employees who are 35 or younger and pairs them with senior executives with whom they meet about once a month. According to Carol Hymowitz in a *Wall Street Journal* article,[110] the executives sometimes learn as much as they teach. The first mentee of Jim Godwin, Senior Vice President of Human Resources was an IT employee who was versed in emerging technologies. "He taught me a lot about new applications and how to train others to use them, even though I'm pretty tech-savvy."

41. ONGOING MENTORING

Pal's Sudden Service is a drive-thru restaurant based in Tennessee. The company uses a 60-point psychometric survey to ensure the teenagers they hire meet their values. The teenagers then receive more than 120 hours of training and on-going mentoring. According to Jeanne Bliss in *Would You Do That to Your Mother*, their turnover is one-third of the industry average and they have lost just seven general managers in 33 years.[111] Leadership is committed to ongoing mentoring. Each team member spends 10 percent of their time daily mentoring team members on a skill or aptitude.

---

110. https://www.wsj.com/articles/the-tricky-task-of-managing-the-new-multigenerational-workplace-1534126021
111. https://www.amazon.com/Would-You-That-Your-Mother/dp/0735217815

In *Generations at Work*,[112] the authors shared that at **KPMG**, every young worker is expected to have a mentor, and middle level employees may be both a mentor and a mentee. KPMG has a website dedicated to mentoring where they promote social activities like lunches, softball games, and happy hours as venues for mentoring. They reduced turnover from 25 percent to 18 percent in five years.

42. STEERING COMMITTEES

Jim Holz, Director of Client Services at **MSA Professional Services**[113] shared how the company created a Next50 Steering Committee for younger professionals. Here is an excerpt from their Charter:

> I. PURPOSE
>
> The purpose of the Next50 Steering Committee is to create and foster a work environment that is engaging and fulfilling, and promotes the success of MSA Professional Services through the lens of the young professional.
>
> II. CORE FUNCTIONS
>
> The Next50 Steering Committee will have five Core Functions:
>
> • Assist, personnel within MSA on young professional ideologies and reactions to corporate policy
>
> • Educate, young professionals on MSA culture, business practices and core values to show how they fit into the greater scope of the industry

112. https://www.amazon.com/Generations-Work-Managing-Boomers-Workplace/dp/0814432336
113. https://www.msa-ps.com/

- Introduce, young professional ideas and policy to MSA

- Retain, young professionals within MSA to create a stable base to transition towards the future

- Attract, young professionals outside of MSA to build on that stable base

According to Holz, "This group regularly conducts "listening sessions" at each of our offices to learn what is on the minds of the younger generation professionals. In the last year, we went away from annual performance evaluations to a monthly check-in format instead, based on recommendations from the Next50."

43. CREATING LISTENING POSTS

Michelle Tunney, Operations Chief at **CuriousityCX,** shared how multi-channel employee listening posts are employed by companies that lead their industries in employee engagement. An engaged employee will be comfortable enough to question authority and will provide spectacularly useful insight in doing so. Make it possible for Gen X employees to complete a survey, speak candidly with leaders directly, attend town hall meetings, or provide anonymous feedback online, and you will tap into the mind of an engaged workforce. Now, if you analyze that feedback, acknowledge it to your workforce, respond and resolve issues appropriately, you will reinforce that engagement and reap immense value. Jamie Notter and Maddie Grant in *When Millennials Take Over* share three examples of companies that are listening to employees uniquely:[114]

> **REI** offers an online "company campfire" a social media/blog-type communication tool that sits on their

114. https://www.amazon.com/When-Millennials-Take-Over-Ridiculously/dp/1940858127

company intranet. 40 percent of employees regularly engage through that forum.

The **Cheesecake Factory** has a Wow Stories initiative, through which anecdotes of exceptional customer service are circulated throughout the company to share best practices and increase employee morale. In order to share these anecdotes, leadership must first make it possible for employees and customers to share those experiences, which reflects the company's commitment to listening.

A junior teller at **TD Bank** expressed frustration internally about a paper-based process that she thought could be better done online, and when many employees echoed that same sentiment on the bank's internal networking site, the company took notice and changed the process. That's using digital technology (and the digital mindset) to enable innovation and continuous improvement.

44. FACE TIME IS IMPORTANT

Mark Beal shared in his book *Decoding Gen Z*[115] the importance of human interaction. He wrote, "In fact, they are craving more of what I like to call H.I. (Human Interaction). Fifty-three percent of Generation Z said they prefer in-person discussion at the workplace. All Gen Zers [whom] I interviewed emphasized the need for more face-to-face time at work, especially with mentors and colleagues, more time in-person with a network of peers and other individuals who share a common purpose and passion and even more time with companies and brands via unique opportunities and experiences." Generation Z wants to collaborate with others

---

115. https://www.amazon.com/Decoding-Gen-Generation-Corporate-Marketers/dp/1724080881

face-to-face in a meaningful way to learn, grow, and evolve. In a survey of 5,000 Gen Zers from more than 100 colleges by Door of Clubs,[116] 37 percent of respondents noted health care benefits were the most important benefit, closely followed by a mentorship program at 33 percent. Mentorship was even more important for Gen Z than time-off and being able to work remotely.

FEEDBACK AND MENTORING TAKEAWAY

Create an open environment of learning and sharing.

Let's now look at Retention and Loyalty ...

---

116. https://medium.com/@doorofclubs/what-5-000-gen-zers-tell-us-about-the-future-of-work-6dd00f796e8f

CHAPTER 18

RETENTION AND LOYALTY

"The long-term success of any company depends heavily upon the quality of its workers and [their] loyalty."

– Timothy Keiningham

Keeping employees engaged is paramount. Retention and loyalty are the cornerstones to any business. Here are nine companies that do the little extra to retain employees across the generations.

45. DIFFERENT STROKES FOR DIFFERENT GENERATIONS

Scripps Health in San Diego wanted to reduce first-year turnover to 15 percent (and overall to six percent). They launched an aggressive campaign to get to know their employees via focus groups, surveys, and interviews. They really listened and figured out that their managers were using a "one-size-fits-all" approach, and their programs (development, benefits, and recruiting) were geared for the "typical employee." They found different generations need different things and trained all their leaders on different communication styles, motivators and de-motivators, and specific leadership strategies. First-year turnover dropped by 8.5 percent. From the book *Generations at Work*,[117] Scripps rolled out perks that "help contribute to a fun, rewarding and appreciative work environment" including onsite day care (Millennials and Gen X), entertainment discounts (all), tuition reimbursement, adoption benefits (Millennials and Gen X), massage, a concierge program, staged retirement (Boomers), wellness assessment and retiree health insurance (Boomers). Did it make an impact? Revenues increased $130 million and *Great Place to Work* scores increased from 58 to 82 in five years.

46. HONOR WORK-LIFE BALANCE

The book *Ties to Tattoos* shared how **REI** respects the work-life balance of its Gen X and Millennial employees.[118] One perk they

---

117. https://www.amazon.com/Generations-Work-Managing-Boomers-Workplace/dp/0814432336

118. https://www.amazon.com/Ties-Tattoos-Generational-Differences-Competitive-ebook/dp/B004X34M40

offer is a 30 percent discount on trips booked through them and a four-week sabbatical. REI was ranked #1 in work-life balance.

47. EMPHASIZE CULTURE

Assurance, a Schaumburg, Illinois, based insurance brokerage, has a whole host of incentives for its employees, including Starbucks coffee, yoga classes, and a Wii station, plus big-ticket items such as referral bonuses for new clients, education reimbursements, and companywide bonuses for reaching goals. Yet the benefits with the biggest impact on culture seem to be those that bring employees together. "I think we're really thoughtful about the things we emphasize," says Jackie Gould, the company's Chief Operating Officer. "A lot of [the benefits] aren't really about the money. It's more about fostering the relationships." According to Steven Handmaker, CMO at Assurance, culture is the secret sauce. Each year the company rallies around a theme and an accompanying song. The songs are typically from the 1980s with a fun/irreverent feel. In 2017, it was the *Power of Love* by Huey Lewis. The previous year was Salt-N-Pepa's, *Push It*, and the theme was wellness.[119] Their Shared Success bonus program is based on four components, two of which are financial and two tie in with the year's cultural theme. For example, during the wellness year, everyone in the company would achieve success if 84 percent of the company completed a 5K race at some point during the year. Over 95 percent ended up completing a race. In 2017, the metric was handwritten notes. Twenty were meant for customers and 17 for friends/family. Over the last few years, Assurance has become a fixture on *Fortune*, Best Place to Work (for Small to Medium businesses), and they won "Best Place to Work in

---

119. https://www.forbes.com/sites/stanphelps/2018/05/02/
micro-weird-your-brand-to-differentiate-in-business-like-trader-joes-assurance-and-magic-castle/

Chicago" by the *Chicago Tribune*.[120] Not bad for a "boring" insurance brokerage.

48. KEEP IT FUN

Featured in the book *Work with Me*, authors Debra Magnuson and Lora Alexander share how **Google** has put a particular emphasis on recruiting and retaining Gen X employees.[121] They adopted the philosophy that "[w]ork should be challenging and the challenge should be fun." They ask their employees to solve hard problems and at the same time, they provide them with free food, onsite chefs, swimming pools, low-price haircuts, subsidized massage, and pool tables.

49. RETAIN FROM WITHIN

Make sure the employees you have know what opportunities you have internally, because new jobs are only a screen away. One of the big differences between generations is how easily the Millennials can find out about job opportunities. Featured in *Sticking Points*[122] by Haydn Shaw, **Marriott** uses technology to enable employees to register for the jobs they would be interested in and notifies them when jobs are available. Shaw shares two additional examples with MITRE Corp and FactSet Research:

MITRE Corp allows employees to "change jobs without changing employers." They encourage internal transfers and encourage managers to offer 8-10 percent of staff to switch jobs each year. Workers of all ages take advantage to gain broader experience.

---

120. http://www.chicagotribune.com/business/careers/topworkplaces/ct-top-workplaces-2016-midsize-assurance-1111-biz-20161111-story.html

121. https://www.amazon.com/Work-Me-Leading-Multigenerational-Workforce-ebook/dp/B001LRPNJE

122. https://www.amazon.com/Sticking-Points-Generations-Working-Together/dp/1414364717

Financial software company **FactSet Research** makes it easy for employees to find new opportunities. They hold career fairs for employees.

50. EMPOWERING EMPLOYEES

Google, **3M**, and **Genetech** all use a similar approach to attract and retain Millennials and Gen X. At Google, they offer "20-percent time." That is, you can use 20 percent of your time to work on personal projects that the company funds and supports. It ties to their purpose of tech enablement.

RETENTION AND LOYALTY TAKEAWAY

Engage employees and show that you care. Set your values and trust your employees to make the right decisions.

PART III

THE GENERATIONAL MATRIX

CHAPTER 19

GENERATIONAL MATRIX

*"The more you know yourself,
the more patience you have
for what you see in others."*

– Erik Erikson, psychologist and author

GRAY GOLDFISH GENERATIONAL MATRIX

EMPLOYEES

	MATURES BORN PRIOR TO 1946	BOOMERS BORN 1946 - 1964
MATURES	**RECRUIT:** Schedule flexibility **TRAIN:** Classroom **MANAGE:** Enlist them to train others **INSPIRE:** Share experiences	**RECRUIT:** Company integrity **TRAIN:** Facts & figures **MANAGE:** Explain how projects help others **INSPIRE:** Emphasize team
BOOMERS	**RECRUIT:** Status they'll have in the organization **TRAIN:** Full of information **MANAGE:** Provide face time to senior leaders **INSPIRE:** Share keys to climbing ladder	**RECRUIT:** Team-oriented business **TRAIN:** Workshops **MANAGE:** Highlight team successes **INSPIRE:** Show how work helps community
GEN X	**RECRUIT:** Share that ideas will be respected **TRAIN:** Summarize, then detail **MANAGE:** Understand the challenges **INSPIRE:** Provide autonomy	**RECRUIT:** Promotion opportunities **TRAIN:** Interactive **MANAGE:** Don't micromanage **INSPIRE:** Earn time off
MILLENNIALS	**RECRUIT:** Opportunity for mentoring **TRAIN:** Let them practice **MANAGE:** Assign small projects first **INSPIRE:** Offer path to promotion	**RECRUIT:** Appeal to their parents **TRAIN:** After-training mentors **MANAGE:** Be open to new ideas **INSPIRE:** Get to know them
GEN Z	**RECRUIT:** Highlight your culture **TRAIN:** Bi-directional mentoring **MANAGE:** Allow worktime flexibility **INSPIRE:** Listen to their tech ideas	**RECRUIT:** Speak to brand purpose **TRAIN:** Mentor, without all the detail **MANAGE:** Let them work start to finish **INSPIRE:** Continuous learning

LEADERS

GENERATION X BORN 1965 - 1979	MILLENNIALS BORN 1980 - 1996	GENERATION Z BORN 1997 AND AFTER
RECRUIT: Show organizational commitment to being #1 **TRAIN:** Summarize **MANAGE:** Be decisive **INSPIRE:** Explain how you'll win	**RECRUIT:** Value their experience **TRAIN:** Patience **MANAGE:** Spell out what's expected **INSPIRE:** Ask for their input	**RECRUIT:** Alleviate fear of tech **TRAIN:** Explain every step **MANAGE:** Don't count on evenings **INSPIRE:** Show you're working hard too
RECRUIT: Opportunity to shine **TRAIN:** At-your-own-pace **MANAGE:** Allow autonomy **INSPIRE:** Provide details of your plan	**RECRUIT:** Respect past achievements **TRAIN:** Interactive team building **MANAGE:** Share all the credit **INSPIRE:** Help them learn	**RECRUIT:** Show they'll be leading edge **TRAIN:** Focus on soft skills **MANAGE:** Ask them to stay late for big projects **INSPIRE:** Ask for their perspective
RECRUIT: Show how organization is different from others **TRAIN:** Computer-based **MANAGE:** Do your share of the work **INSPIRE:** Work/life balance	**RECRUIT:** Opportunity to do different things **TRAIN:** Role play **MANAGE:** Try to make work easier **INSPIRE:** Fun at work	**RECRUIT:** Highlight lack of bureaucracy **TRAIN:** Self-directed **MANAGE:** Specific goals **INSPIRE:** Give them credit
RECRUIT: Flexible scheduling **TRAIN:** Online **MANAGE:** Check in often **INSPIRE:** Explain importance of work	**RECRUIT:** What you like about the organization **TRAIN:** Multi-tasking interaction **MANAGE:** Celebrate small successes **INSPIRE:** Positive feedback	**RECRUIT:** Highlight your tech **TRAIN:** Connect them with their peers **MANAGE:** Face-to-face feedback **INSPIRE:** Schedule flexibility
RECRUIT: Use tech to communicate **TRAIN:** Mentor, don't tell **MANAGE:** Guide in small steps **INSPIRE:** Customize feedback	**RECRUIT:** Wide use of tech **TRAIN:** Collaboratively and with technology **MANAGE:** Enable work/life integration **INSPIRE:** Explain "why"	**RECRUIT:** Promote diversity **TRAIN:** Gamification **MANAGE:** Leverage tech to simplify **INSPIRE:** Tie work to greater purpose

THE GENERATIONAL MATRIX

Now that organizations have five different generations in the workplace and all five of them can be in leadership roles, it's not enough to have tips for "How to Lead Millennials." In order to be an effective leader, we need to know how to lead every generation.

Since we view life through the lens of our own experiences, it's even better to know how to lead every generation *in the context of your own generation.* For instance, we know that Generation X doesn't always enjoy the touchy/feely aspects of leadership. At the same time, Millennials are used to and appreciate more frequent, positive feedback. Those styles don't naturally go together, so Generation X needs to be particularly mindful of how to get the best out of their Millennial employees.

To assist this effort and to provide you with an easy-to-use reference (even though we're sure you'll have this book tabbed and dog-eared), we created the Generational Matrix.

The five generations of leaders are listed across the top. Simply find your generation and then move down the page to find the generation you're leading. Within each cell, you'll see four quick tips on how to recruit, train, manage, and inspire that particular generation. If you think your employee borders on a couple generations, just look at the next cell to the right or left as appropriate. You can also use the matrix in reverse order to coach your manager. (Find your generation from the employee side of the matrix and then move right until you find your manager's generation.)

Let's explore an example from the leadership point of view:

As a Baby Boomer, you're trying to understand how to better lead your Gen Z employees. Find Baby Boomers across the top (second row from the left) and then go to the bottom of the matrix to find the row associated with Generation Z.

From our earlier chapter, you know Gen Z is motivated by purpose so that's a powerful technique to use in **recruiting** them. Speak about how your organization is about more than making money, that there's a greater purpose behind its work and how the new Gen Z employee will be able to contribute to that purpose.

Moving down to the next item in the cell, **training**. As a Baby Boomer manager, you likely have a lot of knowledge to transfer to your Gen Z employee. You'll recall Gen Z is looking for mentors, not managers. A match made in heaven? Maybe, but there's a hurdle you need to overcome as a Baby Boomer: You can't download all your detailed knowledge to your employee. Remember, this is a generation that has never had to look up anything in a book. For many basic inquiries, they just say "Hey, Siri" or "Alexa," ask their question, and receive a concise answer. Gen Z knows every answer isn't that simple, but they're not going to be patient with a long-winded explanation of how things used to be, how things changed, and how things are today. Think brief.

In your day-to-day **managing** of your Gen Z employees, consider letting them stick with projects from start to finish. This isn't easy. While Generation X may be able to lead a project by themselves, Gen Z likely can't. They just haven't had the experience in school (group projects, parents helping) or at home (parents jumping in to save the day). Gen Z will need clear expectations, frequent check-ins, and a little hand holding. Think that's too much effort? Consider this: Who's going to do the detailed grunt work your project requires? You? You're a leader. You need the help your Gen Z employee will provide. And it's your responsibility to help them grow into successful employees and eventual leaders. Little is more demotivating that working on the hardest parts of a project and then watching your leader (that's you, Baby Boomer) present the final result to the senior leadership team. By allowing Gen Z to stick around for the entire project, you'll be growing *and* motivating your employee.

Finally, when it comes to **inspiring** your Gen Z employee, one lever you can pull is one that is near and dear to your heart: continuous learning. Baby Boomers, even near the end of their careers, are interested in learning, whether it be about their organization, their industry, or some new skill they'd like to pick up. As a Boomer, leverage your own passion for learning with Gen Z, a group that is passionate about learning too. This might also be a great opportunity for "reverse mentoring." If you're interested in getting better with using a new technology, maybe presentation software or utilizing social media to greater advantage, ask your Gen Z employee to help. They'll likely jump at the opportunity to have a more meaningful relationship with their manager/mentor and feel like they're making a difference early in their career.

That's just one example of how to utilize the Generational Matrix. There's a cell for every generation of employee you lead. The Generational Matrix will be a handy reminder for how to lead every generation, but let's take a detailed look at how each generation can lead every generation, including their own.

As we've already shown, each generation was shaped in part by their own upbringing, environment, and family. As we conducted our research for this book, however, we learned it's also critical for leaders to understand their own generation. A friend once said, "It's hard to see the label when you're inside the bottle," and that's the case here as well. The more we researched and observed how each generation should lead the others, the more we also learned about how to lead our peers. It's fairly simple to pick out what you like or don't like about the leaders you've followed during your career, but few have taken the time to think through what parts of their generational makeup have caused these preferences. It's for that reason, we'll include every generation in our tips and techniques, including the leader's generation we're highlighting in that section.

CHAPTER 20

MATURE LEADERS

"My parents, products of the Great Depression, were successful people, but lived in a state of constant fear that my sister and I, and they, would sink into the kind of economic insecurity that their generation knew so well."

– Ben Stein, economist, writer, actor, lawyer

TIPS AND TECHNIQUES FOR MATURE LEADERS

MATURE LEADERS
BORN PRIOR TO 1946

MATURES
RECRUIT: Schedule flexibility
TRAIN: Classroom
MANAGE: Enlist them to train others
INSPIRE: Share experiences

BOOMERS
RECRUIT: Share the status they'll have
TRAIN: Full of information
MANAGE: Provide face time to senior leaders
INSPIRE: Share keys to climbing ladder

GEN X
RECRUIT: Share that ideas will be respected
TRAIN: Summarize, then detail
MANAGE: Understand the challenges
INSPIRE: Provide autonomy

MILLENNIALS
RECRUIT: Opportunity for mentoring
TRAIN: Let them practice
MANAGE: Assign small projects first
INSPIRE: Offer path to promotion

GEN Z
RECRUIT: Highlight your culture
TRAIN: Bi-directional mentoring
MANAGE: Allow worktime flexibility
INSPIRE: Listen to their tech ideas

MATURES LEADING MATURE EMPLOYEES

As a member of their generation, you know Mature employees are tough. They're children of the Great Depression, so they know how precious a job can be. Throughout their career, they've worked long hours and put their organization ahead of themselves. As they hit their seventies though, they have a secret they aren't particularly proud of: they're tired of working so hard! They still have the same dedication to a job well done, but they don't want to work fifty hours a week. Some want to spend time with grandkids, some want time to volunteer, and some just want time off. As you are **recruiting** Matures, volunteer that they'll be able to have a flexible schedule and can work less than a full week. Matures won't want to necessarily bring this up on their own, but they'll be relieved to hear you say it. And, as the recruiter/hiring manager, it'll be a great way to bond with your potential employee.

There are several different ways of **training** employees including self-paced, online, and webinar, but to the Mature generation, nothing beats the classroom. As a Mature-generation member yourself, this is a great way to share your knowledge in a way your Matures will appreciate. Another reason the classroom works well for Matures is that they enjoy working and learning in teams. An online portal may make Matures feel isolated in their learning; a classroom will enable them to learn with and from their peers in a comfortable way.

For someone who's been in the workforce for up to fifty years, it's going to feel a little weird to have someone telling them what to do on a daily basis. Matures know they have things to learn, but if they're still working, they likely feel they have more information to give than to receive. That's why one best practice for **managing** Matures is to have them learn the material well enough to teach others. As anyone who has taught knows, you really have to have your arms (and brain) around a subject to teach it. By asking Matures to help teach, you can rest assured that they'll apply their significant work ethic to learning the material and delivering it to the rest of your team. A win-win for everyone involved.

As a Mature leader yourself, you have plenty of experiences to call upon to guide your decisions. Your Mature employees do too. Share your experiences with your Matures and encourage them to do the same with you. Your common memory of how things used to be and leveraging that information to lead your team in the right direction now will be **inspiring** to your Matures and encourage them to bigger and better performance.

MATURES LEADING BABY BOOMER EMPLOYEES

As we emphasized earlier in the book, Baby Boomers care very much about their status within your organization. It matters that they have a respectable title, a nice office, and the respect of their peers, superiors, and subordinates. Those are great aspects of your organization to highlight when **recruiting** a Boomer. Even if you don't have an important title to offer your Baby Boomer recruit, emphasize how their expertise will be appreciated. The Boomer needs to be able to visualize how they'll be empowered to influence the organization positively from their new role.

Baby Boomers love details! They sometimes struggle as leaders/trainers because they like to share all the details of a particular subject with their audience, but when **training** Baby Boomers, more detail is better. For instance, when onboarding a Boomer to a new company, it's not enough to share the summary version of your benefits package. They want the details of exactly what's covered. Likewise, when explaining the company procedures for creating a new product, don't stop at the step-by-step instructions. Also share why those instructions were created, when they were created, and how they've worked successfully in the past. The Boomer's knowledge of the detail and their comfort will move in parallel.

When **managing** any generation, it's important to understand why they work. Certainly, it's the money, but what else is important? For

Baby Boomers, getting recognized is another important element that keeps them going on a daily basis. This doesn't mean star charts like the Millennials; it means face time with upper management. It's not uncommon for Baby Boomers to stay late for an opportunity to "bump into" a senior leader in the hallway. (Some go so far as to wait outside the leader's office with an idea that "just occurred to them.") As their leader, make sure your Boomers get the face time they desire. Even if they're a little lower in your organization, invite them to senior level meetings and give them a speaking role. It'll pay off the next time you ask them to do something more mundane.

While providing face time with senior leaders is a great way to get the most from Baby Boomers on an on-going basis, a key to really **inspiring** them is teaching them how to climb the corporate ladder. As a Mature, you've probably been around your organization for a few years (at least). You know its ins and outs and what buttons to push with different people. Use that wealth of knowledge to inspire your Boomer employees. They'll love the knowledge you can provide and follow your guidance because they are very motivated to continue to earn promotions and broaden their influence within your organization.

MATURES LEADING GENERATION X EMPLOYEES

Generation X was often raised by parents who were either a) concerned about keeping their jobs or b) dealing with a divorce that left them distracted, or c) both! Because of those circumstances, Gen X was often left to fend for themselves. Everyone wants to be appreciated, and because of their background, Gen X especially wants to be heard. In **recruiting** Gen X, highlighting that you'll respect their ideas will go a long way toward them being interested in joining your organization. Step up to be the interested adult in their life that may have been lacking in their childhood, even if we're talking about an employee in their forties.

A common theme with Gen X is they don't like to be bogged down in minutiae. They're used to figuring things out for themselves, and this goes for **training** as well. Start with the big picture with Gen X and see where that leaves you. In many cases, your Gen X employees will nod their heads and get back to work. If you're dealing with a particularly complicated subject, still start with a broad overview and then move into the details. You'll find your Gen Xers will stay engaged and learn the material more quickly.

There's a balance between being left alone to accomplish a task (see "inspiring" below) and being ignored. Just like Gen X wants to know their ideas will be appreciated, they also want to know you're appreciating their effort. When **managing** Gen X, especially during difficult projects, Matures should acknowledge the project's challenges. This will give them an appreciation for what their Gen X employees are achieving (because Gen X isn't inclined to show their work in progress) and to motivate their employees to continue to work hard. Gen X knows the Mature generation is tough to please, in many cases because they were their parents, so a pat on the back from a member of a generation that embraces hard work will go a long way.

The quickest path for **inspiring** a member of Generation X is to give them autonomy. It may seem like always being involved shows you care about them, but Gen X will perceive this as a lack of trust. And, instead of working extra hard to prove you can trust them, Gen X will often start shutting down. "Fine, you want to do this yourself, Mr. Mature? Go for it." The way to inspire your Gen X employee is by showing you believe in them. Give them direction and then step away so they can surprise you with their ingenuity and work ethic.

MATURES LEADING MILLENNIAL EMPLOYEES

Millennials were raised as their parents' friends. Many Millennials, even in their mid-thirties, are in a daily contact with their parents. They yearn for that consistent contact and the guidance they've received for each significant step in their lives. As we shared previously, Millennials' parents sometimes show up for meetings with college academic advisors and for job interviews. When Millennials land their job, however, their parents are no longer there to help them. That's why a major **recruiting** tool for Millennials is to highlight the opportunity they'll have for a mentor at work. Perceived as similar to a parent figure, the mentor is seen as someone who will be there to guide them through important work decisions and help them succeed.

When Matures were young, jobs were scarce, and there wasn't much patience for training. Brian once spoke at a construction company where a member of the Mature generation shared a story from his childhood. His father told him to build a brick wall in a particular location. Told him how long and how tall. And then left for the day. The child had never built a brick wall before, so he did the best he could, but he ultimately failed. At the end of the day, his father came back, saw the poorly-constructed wall, and aggressively berated his son. For Matures, that was on-the-job **training**. For Millennials, though, this would be the absolutely wrong approach. While it might seem counterintuitive to Matures, Millennials will not react well to harsh criticism. And, because they haven't had the opportunity to learn as much on their own (because their parents were usually involved), they need time to practice new skills before trying them in real-life situations. A successful technique for training Millennials is to give them practice scenarios (often online) so they can come up to speed before being under pressure for a "must-have" assignment.

As with their training, it's important to remember the role of a Millennial's upbringing and education when **managing** them on a day-to-day basis. Millennial parents were often involved in their school projects from an early age throughout high school. Likewise, Millennials were taught in school to work in groups even for small projects. That makes them great collaborators but less skilled in leading large projects on their own. For those reasons, a great technique for managing Millennials is to start them on smaller projects that the Mature manager either a) can swoop in and save if necessary or b) can live with less than 100 percent success. This way, Millennials can learn how to manage projects on their own without catastrophic failure should the project not meet all its goals.

Our Millennial chapter opened with "I'm ready to be promoted." Millennial employees have high expectations and little patience when it comes to being promoted. It doesn't make sense to promote an unqualified employee just because they seek promotion. That could be disastrous to an organization. We're not suggesting that. Offering a promotion *path*, however, is still **inspiring** to Millennials without sinking your organization. Share with Millennials the steps (think baby steps) that they should take in the near term to work toward promotion and, at the same time, show them the path to CEO. It may seem crazy for a Mature to have this conversation with a junior employee, but it'll pay dividends. Although it's a hard and narrow one, there actually is a path to the C-suite. You know what it is, so share your knowledge with your Millennials so they can work toward that goal and help your team at the same time.

MATURES LEADING GENERATION Z EMPLOYEES

Though the Mature to Generation Z gap is the largest in the workforce today, the generations do have similarities that can be leveraged for mutual gain. The first is in **recruiting** members of Gen Z. Matures believe in service before self. They were willing to put their lives on the line for their country in World War II like no generation since. Now while Gen Z is not particularly interested in dying for their civilian organization, they are very interested in working for a purpose. Indications are that Gen Z will work for less money for a company they believe in and that is focused on something more than profits. Since Matures are motivated by similar organizational attributes, highlight the aspects of your culture you appreciate in your recruiting conversations with your Gen Z candidates.

Generation Z is starting their first jobs, and they're going to need **training**. Having said that, Matures, they know millions of things you don't. While you've had your head down trying to help your organization succeed, Gen Z has been immersed in technology that can make your life easier. That's why bi-directional mentoring works so well for Mature-Gen Z relationships. Gen Z wants to learn, and they also want to prove their worth. You know down deep that despite "this is how we've always done it," there has to be a better way to achieve some of your goals. By letting Gen Z help, you'll have the opportunity to train them on what they need to know to be successful, and you'll get more efficient at the same time.

Another area when Matures and Gen Z have something in common is the desire for schedule flexibility. Matures have been working hard their entire lives and now want/need flexibility to spend more time with family or for a doctor's appointment. As a Mature, you know you're going to get your work done on time, you'll just do some things during off hours. Even if they haven't proven themselves in your eyes yet, when **managing** Gen Z, we encourage you to afford them the same sort of leniency. Gen Z also wants to have flexibility in their work schedule, and they too will get their work done during "off hours" (though to Gen Z, work and life are much more integrated). Take a chance here, and we bet you'll get more out of your employees.

Like most new employees, Gen Z wants to contribute right away. They're quickly going to see how business is done at your organization and offer suggestions. The trick to **inspiring** this youngest generation is simple—listen. Not every idea is going to be a good one, but Gen Z will have some technology ideas that will make your life easier. And, when you adopt the appropriate ones, Gen Z will be inspired to work harder and then bring you even more ideas that can help carry your organization into the next decade.

CHAPTER 21

BOOMER LEADERS

"The boomers' biggest impact will be on eliminating the term 'retirement' and inventing a new stage of life ... the new career arc."

– Rosabeth Moss Kanter, Harvard Business School

TIPS AND TECHNIQUES FOR BABY BOOMER LEADERS

BOOMER LEADERS
BORN 1946 - 1964

MATURES
RECRUIT: Company integrity
TRAIN: Facts & figures
MANAGE: Explain how projects help others
INSPIRE: Emphasize team

BOOMERS
RECRUIT: Team-oriented business
TRAIN: Workshops
MANAGE: Highlight team successes
INSPIRE: Show how work helps community

GEN X
RECRUIT: Promotion opportunities
TRAIN: Interactive
MANAGE: Don't micromanage
INSPIRE: Earn time off

MILLENNIALS
RECRUIT: Appeal to their parents
TRAIN: After-training mentors
MANAGE: Be open to new ideas
INSPIRE: Get to know them

GEN Z
RECRUIT: Speak to brand purpose
TRAIN: Mentor, without all the detail
MANAGE: Let them work start to finish
INSPIRE: Continuous learning

BABY BOOMERS LEADING MATURES

As a Baby Boomer, you're interested in working for the common good—whether it be social justice, protesting military action, or trying to create a better future for your children. While Matures may not agree with your politics, they do agree with working for an organization that has integrity and puts others before itself. When **recruiting** Matures, this is a point to emphasize. At this stage in their careers, Matures usually have choices about where to work and highlighting your organization as one with integrity will carry weight for them choosing you.

When training new employees, Baby Boomers tend to like to tell a complete story: the history of the organization, why things developed the way they have, and the details of the tasks to be completed. When **training** Matures, think like Sergeant Joe Friday from Dragnet, "Just the facts, ma'am." Matures are no-nonsense learners and prefer facts and figures to long stories. They may come back to learn more about the "why," but at first, give them the "what" and the "how."

While Matures like to be trained with facts and figures, they prefer more context when it comes to why they're working on a particular project. When **managing** Matures, explain how their project and overall effort is helping the company. Matures are comfortable playing a small role in the overall success of an initiative (think the life of a foot soldier in World War II), but they want to know how they're contributing to the overall good of the organization. Reminding them of the important role they play will keep them chugging toward the outcomes you're seeking.

"Service before self" is a mantra Matures hold dear and showing how they're helping their team achieve great things can be an **inspiring** message. As children of the Great Depression, Matures appreciate the value of pulling together to achieve goals, whether it be the survival of the organization or grander outcomes like achieving a revenue goal. Unfortunately, from the Mature point of view, other generations (particularly Generation X) don't naturally gravitate toward working as a team. As a Baby Boomer leader, you can use your natural affinity for teamwork to help your entire organization work together. Your Matures will find additional motivation in this sort of environment and work harder to help achieve your goals.

BABY BOOMERS LEADING BABY BOOMERS

Baby Boomers have always enjoyed working together to achieve goals. No other generation before or since has taken to the streets to provide, en masse, a voice to their concerns about what they considered an unjust war or social inequality. They appreciate working in teams and that's why when a Baby Boomer highlights a team-oriented organization in **recruiting** another Baby Boomer, it carries so much weight. Candidate Boomers will listen to that aspect of a recruiting pitch from another Boomer because they believe they are kindred spirits in the effort to create team successes.

Following the theme of Baby Boomers enjoying team activities, using workshops as the method for **training** Boomers is a powerful technique. Workshops build upon three aspects of the Boomer persona: a) getting face time with influential peers and senior leaders, b) talking through experiences and successes, and c) working together with peers. As a trainer, you'll get much more interpersonal engagement in this training format than you will with other generations and the Boomers will get more out of the training.

There's always a balance between recognizing individuals for a job well done in front of their peers and recognizing the team. If you recognize the individual, they'll be extra motivated, but you may alienate the team. On the other hand, if you recognize the team and one individual did most of the work, you risk alienating your star performer. When **managing** Boomers, lean toward highlighting the team success. Particularly coming from another Boomer, your best individual Boomer performer will appreciate your desire to build a strong team and the team will feel recognized for their contributions.

Whereas other generations will be focused on how their contributions help your organization (and how those contributions may help them get promoted), the **inspiring** message you can send to your Baby Boomers is how their work is helping the community. As a generation of activists, Boomers want to ensure they are working for the common good as well as their organization. By highlighting how they're doing both, you'll give your Boomer employees something to be proud of and to share with their friends and neighbors. And for that, they'll go the extra mile for you.

BABY BOOMERS LEADING GENERATION X

If you're **recruiting** a member of Generation X to your organization that means the candidate/employee is either leaving their mid-career role because they're unhappy or because they've already lost their job. Gen X is not a group of trusting souls, as we have already pointed out, and if they're ready to leave their current situation, they're likely feeling burned by their previous management team. If you want to get them excited about your organization, talk about promotion opportunities. And more so, show them how people in situations similar to theirs have been promoted. Many Baby Boomers will talk about a team-oriented environment because that's what they appreciate. Generation X candidates won't see that necessarily as a plus, they'll want to know what you're going to do for them, and a pay and promotion combination is a compelling place to start.

When it comes to **training** Generation X, your best bet is to make it interactive. As we've just remined you, Gen X doesn't trust management, and as a trainer, you'll be perceived as the voice of management. Baby Boomers generally like to tell stories (dare we say "pontificate") when they train, and this will be perceived as condescending to Gen X audience members. Instead, keep the class entertaining with interactive exercises. This will keep your Gen X employees engaged and keep your Boomer trainers from sounding like they are talking down to the class participants.

Nothing rubs Generation X the wrong way more than micromanaging. They were raised by hard-working, potentially divorced, and sometimes absentee parents and that required them to learn on their own. They figured out how to get started on their own homework, cook their own dinners, and explore different parts of the neighborhood on their bikes. They don't need you looking over their shoulder. When **managing** Gen X, tell them what needs to be done and then quickly move away. If something is absolutely critical to a project's success, make sure they know that, but don't spend time on nuances. Going over a Generation X's PowerPoint slides and changing a "happy" to a "glad" is like nails on a chalkboard. They'll come to you if they need help, and we encourage you to live with largely unimportant stylistic differences.

It may sound simple, but a technique for **inspiring** Generation X is time off when their work is well done. Other generations may want to jump on the next project when the first is finished, but Gen X will appreciate the time off. Gen X finds themselves in a unique time in life: They have aging parents who need cared for and children who need their attention. Every generation feels an obligation to their parents, but Gen X feels an obligation to their children because of the way they were raised. Remember, Gen X didn't receive a lot of attention from their parents, so they are motivated to change that experience. It's just that this "work" thing keeps getting in the way. Give Gen X the time off to take care of their families, and they'll come back motivated to help you.

BABY BOOMERS LEADING MILLENNIALS

OK, we know this is going to sound bizarre, but when **recruiting** Millennials, Baby Boomers should appeal to their parents. You read that right. Depending on where you fall within the Baby Boomer generation, you're roughly the same age as the parents you'll be courting, so you know what matters to them. They want to ensure the very best for their children and aren't afraid of becoming overly involved to make that happen. Play on that desire, invite them to an open house, show how you're going to build upon their hard work to make their children successful. Then, when the Millennial asks their parents what job they should take, you'll have an advocate in the room.

Millennials want mentors. Stats abound about how this is one of the most important aspects of a job for them. At the same time, though, mentoring is very different than **training**. You still have to train Millennials on the basics—the facts and the procedures of their role. Where you can really make a difference, however, is assigning post-training mentors. The mentors will be readily accepted by the Millennials, and they'll be able to show the Millennials how to apply their training to real-life situations. As a Baby Boomer, this will also be a nice chance for you to begin sharing all the valuable information you have locked in your brain.

Baby Boomers are aware and proud of all the steps they've taken to get to this point in their lives. Every time you hear a Millennial talk about skipping a step toward a senior-level position, you cringe, don't you? It's a legitimate desire to want your employees to be prepared for their next role. Having said that, you don't have all the answers. When **managing** Millennials, take time to listen to their ideas and be open to new ways of doing things. Millennials typically have a far better grasp of technology and their expertise may enable you to become more efficient, both as a manager and with your own tasks.

Remember how Millennials were raised as their parents' friends? They're also used to being more casual with adults, sometimes even calling their childhood friends' parents by their first names. When they get to work, however, some of that casualness is gone. They're asked to complete tasks just because their manager asked them to do it, often without an explanation. This is a demotivating disconnect for Millennials. You can overcome this and become an **inspiring** leader for your Millennials through one simple approach: Get to know them as people. Spend time learning about their families, their hobbies, and even their weekend plans. Having this connection with a parental-type figure will make Millennials feel more at home in their job, prompting them to work harder and be less concerned about looking for a new one.

BABY BOOMERS LEADING GENERATION Z

Baby Boomers leading Generation Z is the example we used to show you how to use the Generational Matrix. In case you're using these sections as a reference, we'll repeat it here for your convenience and add some additional detail.

From our earlier chapter, you know that Gen Z is motivated by purpose so use that in **recruiting** them. Speak about how your company is about more than making money, that there's a greater purpose behind its work and how the new Gen Z employee will be able to contribute to that purpose. Purpose is something that resonates with you as a Baby Boomer, so when you speak about it, speak from your heart and your own experience. Your message will come across as meaningful and add even more credence to the greater purpose behind your organization's efforts.

As a Baby Boomer manager, you likely have a lot of knowledge to transfer to your Gen Z employee. Recall that Gen Z is looking for mentors, not managers. A match made in heaven? Maybe, but there's a hurdle you need to overcome as a Baby Boomer **training** Gen Z: you can't onload all your detailed knowledge on your employee. Remember, this is a generation that has never had to look up anything in a book. For many basic inquiries, they just say, "Hey, Siri" or "Alexa," ask their question, and receive a concise answer. Gen Z knows every answer isn't that simple, but they're not going to be patient with a long-winded explanation of how things used to be, how things changed, and how things are today. Think brief.

In your day-to-day **managing** of your Gen Z employee, consider letting them stick with projects from start to finish. This isn't easy. While Generation X may be able to lead a project by themselves, Gen Z likely can't. They just haven't had the experience in school (group projects, parents helping) or at home (parents jumping in to save the day). Gen Z will need clear expectations, frequent check-ins, and a little hand holding. It'll be worth the effort, however, because your Gen Z will have more context and a much bigger picture the next time you assign them a project. The first one may require some hand holding, but they'll be much better with subsequent ones.

When it comes to **inspiring** your Gen Z employee, one lever you can pull is one that is near and dear to your heart: continuous learning. Baby Boomers, even as they near the end of their careers, are interested in learning, whether it be about their company, their industry, or some new skill they'd like to pick up. As a Boomer, leverage your own passion for learning with Gen Z, a group that is passionate about gaining knowledge too. This might also be an opportunity for "reverse mentoring." If you're interested in getting better with using a new technology, maybe presentation software or utilizing social media to greater advantage, ask your Gen Z employee to help. They'll likely jump at the opportunity to have a more meaningful relationship with their manager/mentor and feel like they're making a difference early in their career.

CHAPTER 22

GENERATION X LEADERS

"Do or do not. There is no try."

– Yoda from Star Wars, *The Empire Strikes Back*

TIPS AND TECHNIQUES FOR GENERATION X LEADERS

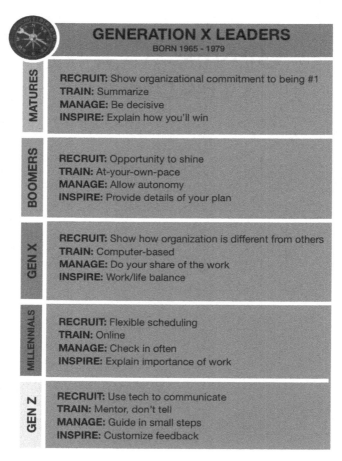

GENERATION X LEADERS
BORN 1965 - 1979

MATURES
RECRUIT: Show organizational commitment to being #1
TRAIN: Summarize
MANAGE: Be decisive
INSPIRE: Explain how you'll win

BOOMERS
RECRUIT: Opportunity to shine
TRAIN: At-your-own-pace
MANAGE: Allow autonomy
INSPIRE: Provide details of your plan

GEN X
RECRUIT: Show how organization is different from others
TRAIN: Computer-based
MANAGE: Do your share of the work
INSPIRE: Work/life balance

MILLENNIALS
RECRUIT: Flexible scheduling
TRAIN: Online
MANAGE: Check in often
INSPIRE: Explain importance of work

GEN Z
RECRUIT: Use tech to communicate
TRAIN: Mentor, don't tell
MANAGE: Guide in small steps
INSPIRE: Customize feedback

GENERATION X LEADING MATURES

Matures care about being the best. They lived (and many served in the armed forces) during World War II where "trying your best" wasn't good enough. You either won or there was a decent chance you were coming home in a body bag. Matures get that the stakes aren't that high in business, but they still care about high achievement. That's why you should highlight your company's commitment to being #1 when **recruiting** Matures. At this stage in their life, they have choices, and a company that strives to be mediocre is not likely one they want to join.

As a member of Generation X, you can't stand wasting time. Meetings that drag on for no reason suck the life out of you, and Matures are the same way. Keep this in mind when **training** Matures by trying to summarize the material as best you can. Clearly, there will be content that requires you to go into detail but think about how you can streamline your approach. By keeping things succinct, you'll earn the respect of your Mature population, and it'll get you on to your next task quickly too.

Growing up in the Great Depression (or at least being greatly influenced by it), there was no time for pondering your many options. When Matures saw a job opportunity, they jumped at it because there were 15 other people vying for the same spot. It's the same with their experience in the military. There wasn't time to sit around discussing various courses of action. You followed the command of your superiors and moved forward, quickly. For these reasons, you should be decisive when **managing** Matures. They'll appreciate your bias toward action and respond in kind.

When recruiting Matures, you'd be wise to highlight your organization's desire to be the best. You should take a similar approach when **inspiring** them to do great things. Explain how you're going to win against the competition and your Mature employees will be fired up (provided your plan isn't a terrible one), They may perceive Gen X (and, really, all younger generations) as not having the same desire to succeed as they had. When you show them how you're motivated to win and have a plan to do it, they'll be much more apt to follow you even if you stumble as a leader from time to time.

GENERATION X LEADING BABY BOOMERS

Any time you're **recruiting** someone from an older generation, they'll be a little concerned that you're more concentrated on your own promotion opportunities than you will be on theirs. This is especially true of Baby Boomers who want to continue to earn positive recognition. Explain to Boomers you'll give them an opportunity to shine, and they'll be more excited about joining your team. Remember, Baby Boomers like details so it's not enough to say you'll make sure they get recognized. You'll need to be specific about how you'll give them the opportunity to present to senior management or let them lead important projects.

When we talked about Baby Boomers **training** Baby Boomers, we said workshops were a great way to enable them to collaborate. But that was because the Boomer trainers also liked that setting. As a Generation X leader, you're going to be less tolerant of sitting in a conference room debating ideas. A good balance between your style and that of your Boomer employee is to offer them at-your-own-pace training. This will allow the Boomer to go through the training slowly or repeatedly if they want and then come to you with questions. It'll be a better use of time for both of you.

Baby Boomers likely have more experience than you do (at least in life, perhaps in your industry as well) so give them autonomy when **managing** them. They will appreciate the feeling of getting to run their own work life, and you'll appreciate the opportunity to get your own work done. "Autonomy" doesn't mean "ignoring," so you'll need to check in at strategic points, but this way your Boomer employee will feel more like they "own" their project and that you respect their experience. Remember, Baby Boomers hold their experience in high regard and your respect of that experience will go a long way with them.

Your Baby Boomer employees were alive in the 1960s when President Kennedy said we would put a man on the moon by the end of decade. They love that sort of far-reaching vision but are also sticklers for details. When **inspiring** Baby Boomers, don't be afraid of shooting for the moon. They'll appreciate the audacious goal—especially when you back it up with the detailed plan for how you're going to make your vision a reality. Let them ask questions about how, together, you'll achieve those goals, and they'll be working hard right alongside you.

GENERATION X LEADING GENERATION X

You know this better than anyone: Generation X distrusts authority. They saw their parents get laid off and don't believe the company rhetoric about how they take care of their employees. As a (cynical) member of Gen X, you can make a positive impact in **recruiting** your (cynical) Gen X candidate by showing how your company is different. Be matter of fact about what the company does well and what it doesn't do so well. When you're genuine about how your company treats its employees differently (even if it's only in specific areas), it will resonate with your Gen X candidate.

Generation X is sensitive about wasting time. When first joining your company, they want to hit the ground running and two days of training "jammed" into five days will kill their spirit. That's why computer-based **training** works well with Gen X. They can quickly click through the parts they already know and still learn new material. This approach works for training employees with new responsibilities and with continuing education as well.

Because of their natural distrust of authority, your Generation X employees are going to be watching you. They're not afraid to think (if not openly express) critical thoughts about your performance. This is especially true if they think you aren't pulling your weight.

If you're in the limelight with senior management and leaving all the hard work to your employees, you'll definitely see morale and motivation dip. When **managing** Gen X, let them see you doing your share of the work. Don't do it in a boastful way, just contribute in an obvious way that helps the team succeed. This will build trust with your employees and keep them working hard for you.

When it comes to **inspiring** Generation X employees, always keep the work/life balance in mind. Gen X employees are at the age where many of them have children at home and because they typically didn't get a lot of time with their parents, they are particularly sensitive to making sure they are involved in their children's lives. That means when it's time to go home, it's time to go home. Likewise, many Gen Xers are starting to deal with aging parents who need additional attention. Their parents may not drive well at night or need some looking after in the evening. In this sandwich of children and parents both needing their attention, Gen X is pulled in many directions. They still want to do a great job at work, but if you recognize their need for a life outside work, they'll put in an even more concentrated effort in the office.

GENERATION X LEADING MILLENNIALS

While Generation X cares deeply about work/life balance, Millennials care deeply about work/life *integration*. As digital natives, they've always been connected with friends, work, and school, so they don't often completely unplug. For that same reason, they don't see why work should be a set time each day (e.g. eight a.m. to five p.m.). In **recruiting** Millennials, talk about how you'll enable them to have a flexible schedule. (Notice we didn't say *allow* them a flexible schedule—don't talk down to them.) Millennials will be attracted to an organization that thinks like they do and, in many cases, put in extra effort during what you would consider "off hours" because you've afforded them some flexibility during the day.

Millennials have been learning online their entire life, and your **training** should embrace that. It's not just that your training is accessed via the web but also that it's available on demand. YouTube has become a source of training videos for everything from cleaning a clogged toilet to how to win video games. It's second nature for Millennials to search for something they want to know, learn it in the moment, and then tackle a task with their newfound knowledge. Instead of having a multi-day class about how to do every aspect of a Millennial's job, give them the big picture and then access to all the online modules they'll need ... when they need them.

In an effort to help their Millennial children succeed, parents were way more involved in their children's lives than any previous generation. Among other things, this meant an active role in school projects and, as we shared before, even job applications. This led to a snowball effect at many schools: projects completed by parents were exceptional, so standards went up which meant the parents needed to be even more involved in the next project. The good news is that the parent/student team produced some awesome work. The bad news is the students didn't learn to do it for themselves. This shortcoming rears its ugly head when Millennials start leading their own projects at work. When **managing** Millennials, Generation X leaders need to check in frequently to ensure their Millennials are still on the right track and haven't stalled due to lack of guidance. This approach isn't natural for Gen X leaders who would usually prefer to provide initial direction and then step away, but it's essential when leading Millennials.

Nine out of 10 Millennials say that meaning is the most important part of their work. They don't want to work hard on an initiative without understanding how it fits into the bigger picture. **Inspiring** Millennials means taking the time to explain how their piece of the puzzle, no matter how small, is critical to the overall success of your organization. When Millennials see the value of their contribution, you'll get more than just effort on that particular project.

You'll also get them thinking about how to add value in other areas. This energy and creativity will pay off for you (and them) many times over.

GENERATION X LEADING GENERATION Z

If you're a Generation X leader with children, you've already experienced the fact that Generation Z does not respond to what you would consider normal forms of communication. First, they probably rarely check email. If you call them, they may not answer. If you text, they'll get your message, but may not respond. If you send them something on Snapchat, they'll respond in seconds. These are the same lessons you can apply when **recruiting** Gen Z. They're either going to be slow to respond to your normal outreach (particularly email) and/or they're going to think you are an antiquated organization that won't be fun/exciting to work for. We know this will be outside your comfort zone but reach out to candidates via more high-tech methods and you'll get the response you're hoping for.

Though Generation Z didn't receive all the parental hand-holding that the Millennials did, they still want someone to guide them through their **training**. They want a mentor who shepherds them through projects or organizational politics, not someone who tells them what to do and leaves. As you share the details Gen Z will need to know to do their job well, consider more one-on-one conversations where you can explain the context of the information and its purpose. Obviously, this is more time consuming than en masse training so speaking with Gen Z in small groups can work as well.

Generation Z suffers from some of the same challenges the Millennials face: they had a lot of help as children and didn't always learn to lead projects on their own. The difference, though, is that they would prefer to be more independent. When **managing** Gen Z, think of a blend of Gen X and Millennials. Give them some of the independence that you, as a member of Gen X appreciate, but also give them small steps that lead to the end goal. Gen Z won't appreciate the frequent feedback Millennials crave, but they also can't be left alone for long stretches of time. By providing them a series of short-term goals, they'll feel more independent, continue to learn, and you'll get the results you want.

Nearly everything has been customized in the lives of Generation Z. They can pick the songs they want without buying the whole album, they're separated into smaller learning groups at school based on their abilities, and they can build their own worlds/teams in video games. **Inspiring** them also takes a customized approach. When it comes to feedback and career guidance, Gen Z will bristle at a one-size-fits-all approach. They want you to think through their individual circumstance and provide leadership that appears to be specifically for them. As a leader, it's perfectly okay to take lessons learned from your own experience—either personally or when leading others—because no employee is truly unique. The key is to communicate in a way that feels like your feedback and advice is exclusively for your Gen Z employee.

CHAPTER 23

MILLENNIAL LEADERS

"Leadership is not about the next election,
it's about the next generation."

– Simon Sinek, author of *Start With Why*
and *Leaders Eat Last*

TIPS AND TECHNIQUES FOR MILLENNIAL LEADERS

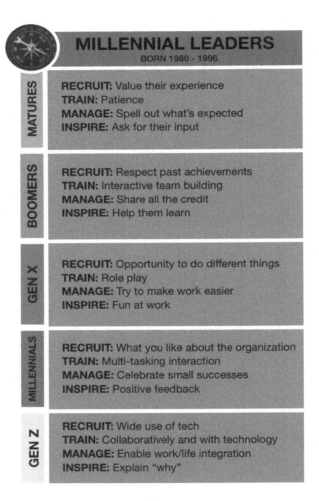

MILLENNIAL LEADERS
BORN 1980 - 1996

MATURES
RECRUIT: Value their experience
TRAIN: Patience
MANAGE: Spell out what's expected
INSPIRE: Ask for their input

BOOMERS
RECRUIT: Respect past achievements
TRAIN: Interactive team building
MANAGE: Share all the credit
INSPIRE: Help them learn

GEN X
RECRUIT: Opportunity to do different things
TRAIN: Role play
MANAGE: Try to make work easier
INSPIRE: Fun at work

MILLENNIALS
RECRUIT: What you like about the organization
TRAIN: Multi-tasking interaction
MANAGE: Celebrate small successes
INSPIRE: Positive feedback

GEN Z
RECRUIT: Wide use of tech
TRAIN: Collaboratively and with technology
MANAGE: Enable work/life integration
INSPIRE: Explain "why"

MILLENNIALS LEADING MATURES

"Kids these days don't appreciate how hard things used to be," said older people many times. It's hard to break them from that impression and even harder when a young person is going to be their manager. As a Millennial **recruiting** Matures, one of the first things you need to communicate is how you value their experience. One of the reasons you're recruiting them in the first place is that they have attributes and experience you appreciate. Highlight those in the recruiting process. This isn't the time to play hard ball. Instead, be open about the value you think they can bring to your organization. It'll be a great first step toward landing the person you want for your team.

Matures can bring an important set of experiences to your team, but those experiences probably don't align perfectly with yours. For confident leaders, it's a good thing to surround yourself with different talents. However, it also means you're likely going to need to train them on the parts of your organization they aren't familiar with. When **training** Matures, you'll have to be patient especially when it comes to technology. Even the most savvy Matures aren't going to have the same tech skills you do. They might not be comfortable searching for answers on the Internet or using a smartphone app to track their progress. Since these activities are second nature to you, your patience will be critical in bringing your Mature employee up to speed on what they need to know.

Ambiguity is going to be a trouble spot in **managing** Matures. When Matures entered the workforce, they had a boss who told them what to do—usually in a very direct manner. They were given specific goals, and they put in specific, dedicated effort to achieve those goals. Ever go to dinner with someone from the Mature generation? They'll ask you the night before when they should be ready to leave and then be ready 10 minutes before that time, looking at their watches. When you saunter down the stairs 5 minutes late, you're thinking it's no big deal and they're irritated. The same goes for work. If you give Matures wildly open-ended directions (something you may like), they'll be uncomfortable. Instead, clearly spell out what's expected of them and they'll deliver.

So far, we've talked about how your default leadership style may make Matures uncomfortable. They know they bring a lot to your organization, but they also want to fit in. By asking for their input on decisions, you'll be **inspiring** them to continue bringing positive energy to your team. "This kid actually cares what I have to say!" they'll think and with that perspective they'll be more willing to share good ideas. Matures have succeeded and failed hundreds more times than you have. When you ask them to weigh in with their experiences, they'll save you from having to learn all those lessons yourself.

MILLENNIALS LEADING BABY BOOMERS

As Millennials, you want to get ahead in your organization and prove your worth. If you're able to skip a career step or spend less time in a role that's lower on the organizational chart than others, all the better. For Baby Boomers, every step of their career matters. Most Boomers have plaques and certificates proudly displayed in their offices commemorating those past achievements. That's why when **recruiting** Baby Boomers, it's particularly powerful to respect their past achievements. When you point out how you value certain achievements on a Boomer's resume, they'll feel confident you'll do the same when they work for you.

Baby Boomers and Millennials have a few attributes in common and one of them is enjoying working with teams. In addition, since Boomers raised Millennials as their friends, the two generations enjoy working on the same team. Interactive team building is a best practice for **training** Baby Boomers that Millennials also appreciate. Getting the two groups together to learn new material in a fun environment will ingrain the topic in Boomers' brains while also making them feel better about their team—and its leader.

Even if Baby Boomers may be on the downside of their career (and if they're being managed by someone decades their junior, they probably are), they still want to be recognized for their achievements. When **managing** them, share the credit for a team success. It doesn't matter if they played a smaller role and you did most of the work. Your Boomers will appreciate the recognition and at the same time appreciate you as a leader. They're savvy enough to know you did the majority of the work, but when you still give them credit, they'll work harder next time to ensure they earn it.

Baby Boomers are lifetime learners. They like to read about the latest in their industry and try new technology. The key to **inspiring** them is to help them on their learning journey. Email them articles you found interesting and might help them do their job more efficiently. Send them to a conference or offsite training course, and then ask them to share what they learned with your team when they return to the office. They'll be fired up to learn and fired up to share their new-found knowledge.

MILLENNIALS LEADING GENERATION X

Millennials and Generation X don't have many things in common, but there is one area where they typically do and it can be used as a good **recruiting** tool. Both Millennials and Gen X appreciate variety in their work so that's an item to highlight to Gen X candidates. Impress upon your future Gen X employees that they'll have the opportunity to learn and do different things with you as their leader. This may mean interacting with multiple departments or learning a new skill that will help their career. Remember, Gen X doesn't really trust their employer, so honing capabilities that will help them as an individual (in a potential future role) will carry more weight than sharpening capabilities that will only help in the specific role for which they're being considered.

Growing up, Generation X had to create a lot of their own fun. They had less parental guidance and structured play (there was no such thing as a "play date") during their free time, so they used their imagination. You can take advantage of this when **training** Gen X by utilizing role plays. Role playing scenarios employees may encounter—especially in sales—is often an effective tool, but other generations bristle at the artificial nature of the role play. Gen X is more likely to embrace the role play and get the most out of the training.

Being as efficient as possible is of major importance to Generation X so when **managing** them, try to make the work as easy as possible. This doesn't mean only giving Gen X easy tasks to accomplish. It means eliminating roadblocks and cutting down on the bureaucracy as much as possible. Gen X will follow your lead if you free them from what they perceive as meaningless activities (like largely-worthless meetings) and enable them to focus on their work. If there is a software program that eliminates manual labor, install it. If you can communicate a senior leadership update in an email instead of a 60-minute meeting, write it. Your Gen X employee will recognize your efforts to streamline their work lives and appreciate you for them.

Generation X was the first generation to intentionally add fun to their work schedules. This is the generation that brought NCAA basketball pools and fantasy football to the workplace. You'll be effective **inspiring** them when you do some of the same. To our point in the paragraph above, don't make your "fun" feel like extra work, but when you add some competition or laughter to your team, Gen X will be motivated to work harder. Millennials enjoy working as a team so use your team-first inclination to devise fun team building events. You'll help your team grow closer while you inspire your Gen X employees.

MILLENNIALS LEADING MILLENNIALS

As members of the same generation, **recruiting** Millennials will be easier than with other generations. Just tell them what you like about your organization. If you're not sure what to emphasize, think through the attributes Millennials appreciate about a company. Things like working as a team, flexible schedules, mentoring, and the ability to get promoted. All of these characteristics will resonate with your Millennial candidates and your sincerity about your organization will help seal the deal.

You know Millennials are great at multi-tasking. They can watch TV, work on an assignment, and listen to music while eating a snack. They don't like doing things in serial so make sure your **training** has a multi-tasking element to it as well. You can create a podcast with training material your Millennials can listen to while completing another assignment. Or, give them pre-workshop video modules they can complete at home while cooking dinner. Our older generations are reading this saying, "You can't do that, they'll never learning anything." As a Millennial, though, you know this is the way not only to teach your employees but also to motivate them to complete the training in a timely fashion.

Millennials grew up with refrigerator star charts celebrating minor accomplishments throughout the day. When **managing** Millennials, you'll be successful doing something similar. No, you don't have to have star magnets outside your office, but you do need to celebrate small successes. Millennials don't have the stamina to wait for the end of a 6-month project to receive praise. They need it early and often to stay motivated. Presentations to senior leaders deserve a kudo. Finishing a step in the project plan gets a pat on the back. Even a good idea receives an email of thanks. While these rewards take time out of your day, they'll pay huge dividends when it comes to keeping your Millennials on the right track.

As with celebrating small successes, providing positive feedback can be used for **inspiring** Millennials. More than just a pat on the back, your feedback should be detailed and specific about how your employee is helping the organization. Point out the skills they're employing (particularly if they're recently learned), the results they're achieving, and how they are progressing toward a higher level of importance in the organization. As a Millennial leader, it's easy to get a little depressed about how long it takes to get promoted in your organization, so be careful to be upbeat when speaking with your employees. Having said that, it's okay to share developmental feedback as well. Millennials appreciate a slant toward the positive, but you must communicate where Millennials need to grow too. Despite everything you read, your Millennial employee will be able to handle that feedback and even will embrace it if you couple it with the things they're doing right.

MILLENNIALS LEADING GENERATION Z

Generation Z has had the opportunity to customize a large portion of their lives. They can create playlists, stream only the shows they want to watch, and even design customized college courses. When they start looking for jobs, they'll be disappointed about how each job description looks so static. That is, until they get to yours! When **recruiting** Gen Z, point out the aspects of the role that can be customized to their liking. Perhaps it's having a choice about their career path (almost any new hire has choices) or the order of their onboarding training. Gen Z will feel more at home with your organization even before they accept the job.

Two things are abundant in the scholastic lives of Generation Z: working in groups and using technology to learn. Almost all schools have at least some assignments where students write papers or present projects as a team. Gen X had very little of this and will push employees toward individual effort, but as a Millennial leader, you can leverage some of your own experiences to facilitate group **training**. As mentioned, technology was also a critical part of Gen Z learning. Members of Gen Z watched *Minecraft* videos as kids and continue to watch *Fortnight* videos for ways to improve their skills. When you align your training with activities Gen Z is already used to, they'll pay closer attention and learn more quickly.

While previous generations were interested in work/life balance, you'll want to think through work/life *integration* when **managing** Generation Z. Gen Z is used to being continuously connected to their friends via social media, so leverage that propensity by enabling them to work from wherever they are. If they can contribute to their job via an app, they'll do it while waiting in line for lunch (because, like you, they're great multi-taskers). Make sure they have the programs and connectivity they need to accomplish tasks from home. This may mean providing them a high-end Wi-Fi router or giving them a stipend for higher bandwidth Internet. Enabling this flexibility will get you the results you want while also keeping your Gen Z employees' morale high.

More than any generation before it, Generation Z wants to know why they're working on a specific project or task, and you can be **inspiring** to them when you take the time to provide those details. Start big and then walk your employee through how their work contributes to the purpose or vision of the company. Share how they are contributing to the team and why their individual piece is important. It's also beneficial to share why you think the approach you've suggested (mandated) is the right one. When doing this, stay open to ideas because your Gen Z employee may have suggestions for how to make the task easier. When you change your thinking based on their recommendation, you'll inspire them even more!

CHAPTER 24

GENERATION Z LEADERS

"The people who work for you aren't building a company for you, they are building it for themselves— they are the center of their own universe. Just because you are the CEO doesn't mean they are coming to work every day to make you happy."

– Ben Lerer, CEO Thrillist Media Group

TIPS AND TECHNIQUES FOR GENERATION Z LEADERS

GENERATION Z LEADERS
BORN 1997 AND AFTER

MATURES

RECRUIT: Alleviate fear of tech
TRAIN: Explain every step
MANAGE: Don't count on evenings
INSPIRE: Show you're working hard too

BOOMERS

RECRUIT: Show they'll be leading edge
TRAIN: Focus on soft skills
MANAGE: Ask them to stay late for big projects
INSPIRE: Ask for their perspective

GEN X

RECRUIT: Highlight lack of bureaucracy
TRAIN: Self-directed
MANAGE: Specific goals
INSPIRE: Give them credit

MILLENNIALS

RECRUIT: Highlight your tech
TRAIN: Connect them with their peers
MANAGE: Face-to-face feedback
INSPIRE: Schedule flexibility

GEN Z

RECRUIT: Promote diversity
TRAIN: Gamification
MANAGE: Leverage tech to simplify
INSPIRE: Tie work to greater purpose

GENERATION Z LEADING MATURES

If you're a member of Generation Z **recruiting** Matures, you're in a unique situation and likely trying to attract a very unique Mature. It's not common that someone wants to work for a leader who is fifty-five years their junior! Having said that, there may be circumstances where you want the Mature perspective. As unique as your target audience may be, they're still not going to have anywhere close to your comfort level with technology. Alleviate their fear of the technology you're using by promising to either a) keep them clear of it or b) teach them how to use it. Explicitly address it in your recruiting process. If your Mature candidate wants to learn the latest tech, great (they probably won't). If they want to avoid it, tell them that's okay too.

As a member of Generation Z, you grew up with fewer instructions than previous generations. As we previously shared, you're the generation that got the new iPhone and played with it until you figured out how it worked. There were no directions, and you wouldn't have read them anyway. When **training** Matures, you'll have to change your style. They're used to following directions and will want you to walk them through every step of their new role. Even though you are significantly younger than they are, every employee wants to impress their manager. Your Matures will be uncomfortable if their training doesn't enable them to do that.

It's expected in this day and age for employees to be available outside of the office. To Matures, though, this is an alien concept. They'll work hard for you from eight to five, but when the "whistle blows," they're done and on their way to enjoying their evening. Don't expect Matures to be connected to their phones or checking email at night. When **managing** Matures, it's safe to assume they are unavailable until the next morning (or Monday in the case of a weekend). As an aside, we ask that the Gen Z leaders reading this take a moment to follow this link (www.youtube.com/watch?v=uq7noaMwLfg) to the intro of the Flintstones cartoon on YouTube to see how a Mature reacts when they're notified their work day is complete. Just watch the first 39 seconds—you'll get the picture.

Matures are known for their incredible work ethic and (hate to break it to you), younger generations are not. This belief is exacerbated when the Mature can't see you doing the work (as in if you do it from home). Having said that, you'll be **inspiring** to your Mature employees when you show them you're working hard too. Share the challenges you're overcoming and the work you've accomplished. You'll have to be careful that you don't look like a showoff, so insert what you've accomplished into the context of everyone doing their share to advance the project or company. Since Matures won't be working at night, they'll be impressed with what you accomplish during your "off" hours.

GENERATION Z LEADING BABY BOOMERS

Whether you know it or not, as a Generation Z leader, you're on the leading edge of the next generation of ideas. Your complete comfort with technology and how you approach problem solving is unique to business. Play this up when **recruiting** Baby Boomers. Boomers like to learn new, better ways of doing things and will be attracted to what you can teach them. Don't go so far as to suggest that your Baby Boomer candidate doesn't already have great skills. Instead, talk about how you're going to enhance that skillset.

It may seem miles apart, but your experience achieving "**training**" milestones as a Generation Z leader aligns well with how Baby Boomers like to recognize their accomplishments. The reason we have training in quotes is because you didn't think it was training. At this point, nearly every member of Gen Z has played *Fortnite* or a similar online game. As you progress through the game's challenges, you earn new "skins" (what your character looks like on the screen) or other awards. In essence, you're rewarded for learning how to advance in the game and appreciate the symbolism of that award. Baby Boomers are the same way. They probably don't play *Fortnite*, but as we pointed out earlier in the book, they love to receive recognition—in the form of plaques and certificates—for advancing to the next stage of their education. Get creative with how you reward your Baby Boomers for accomplishing their training and make sure you give them something they can hang on their wall as a symbol of their achievement.

This is going to sound alien, but stay with us for a second. When **managing** Baby Boomers, intentionally set up an early evening meeting with them where they'll get a chance to present something to a senior leader. "Why not just do it during the day?" you ask. That's because it won't seem as special to your Boomer if all the other employees are still around the office. By creating an opportunity for your Boomer to stay late with a senior leader, you'll be rewarding them for their hard work with valuable face time. As a Gen Z leader, this approach is likely not in your comfort zone, but it will pay dividends with your Baby Boomer employees.

Baby Boomers relish all the steps they've taken to reach this point in their careers. They've learned lessons along the way and are excited to share them. At the same time, they're aware that their Generation Z leader probably doesn't want to hear their antiquated stories. You can resolve this internal conflict and be **inspiring** to your Baby Boomer at the same time by asking for their perspective. Ask them to tell you about a time where they faced a similar challenge to the one you're facing now. Ask about the lessons they learned and how to apply them to today's environment. Your Boomer will be thrilled about the opportunity to share, motivated to help you meet your goals, and they may even have some great ideas.

GENERATION Z LEADING GENERATION X

As a Generation Z leader, you're an expert at making things as efficient as possible. Highlight these efficiencies and lack of bureaucracy when **recruiting** Generation X. Even though Gen X isn't as comfortable about work/life integration as you are, they are absolutely interested in a work/life balance. Explain to them how you've cut down worthless meetings, created flexible schedules, and worked to streamline processes. They'll immediately be attracted to your organization and to you as their manager.

Self-directed **training** for your Generation X employee will be a good fit for both of you. As we've shared multiple times, Gen X was raised to look out for themselves. They're used to being self-sufficient problem solvers and don't appreciate someone looking over their shoulder. The reason this is such a good approach for a Gen Z leader is because you're used to figuring things out on your own too. It's rare for you to read an instruction manual; you just play with your new device until you figure it out. Being kindred spirits—at least when it applies to training—will enable you to create a curriculum that matches your style and that of your Gen X employee.

Generation X doesn't trust senior leaders in general, and they're going to be a little less trustful of you because you're decades younger than they are. They'll be wondering if you'll evaluate them fairly when it comes to annual appraisal time. That's why when **managing** Gen X, it's in your best interest to provide them with specific goals to achieve. With specific measures, your Gen Xers will be more comfortable that they're working in the right direction, and black and white goals will alleviate their concern that you'll give them a bad grade come appraisal time.

With their distrust of management, **inspiring** Generation X isn't the easiest thing to do. They'll be looking for you to steal the credit for their hard work. As a young leader, we know you want to get ahead in your organization, but you can't do it on the back of Gen X. If you do, it'll just reinforce their distrust. On the opposite side of the spectrum, a huge motivator is to flip that scenario and give them 100 percent credit for their efforts. Your Gen X employee will be pleasantly surprised and look to see if you do it again. When you do, they'll be fired up to support you as a leader and work especially hard on their projects.

GENERATION Z LEADING MILLENNIALS

When older generations promote their use of technology to younger ones, it can feel disingenuous. "Is it really high tech or are they just saying that to make me want to work there?" On the flip side of that coin, Generation Z leaders can make powerful statements about technology when **recruiting** Millennials. Born, raised, and immersed in technology, Gen Z leaders can speak about how technology will make the job easier and enable the Millennials to learn new things while also collaborating with their peers in a productive way. Because it's coming from a younger generation, Millennials are far more likely to believe it.

Both Generation Z and Millennials grew up in social environments. They worked on group projects in school and stayed connected with friends and family via social media. Since both groups are so used to it, **training** Millennials by connecting them with their peers is a great approach. Millennials will want to share what they're learning and compare ideas with their coworkers even if it is remotely. This can be done via small group webinars that enable the Millennials to share best practices as well as approaches that haven't worked so well. As a member of Gen Z, you'll be comfortable with virtual training so your Millennial employees will get the best out of every session.

When it comes to the day-to-day **managing** of Millennials, you may be tempted to employ technology here as well. That approach can certainly work, but when providing feedback, make sure it's face-to-face. Millennials grew up in near-constant contact with their parents and while many of those interactions were via text, the hard ones were done in person. More than any other generation, Millennials are sensitive to developmental (negative) feedback and aren't used to those conversations happening on the phone or via email/text. Sit down with your Millennial employees. Share what you think they're doing well and then offer feedback/suggestions on how they can get better. Taking the time to speak in person will soften the blow that you don't think they're perfect while also getting across the information they need to improve.

As we've shared, Millennials have entered the workplace with high expectations. They expect to be successful quickly and, in turn, be promoted quickly as well. When that doesn't happen, doubt creeps into their brain in two areas: "Am I really not as good as I think I am?" and "Do my leaders not trust me?" As a leader, you can either double down on these perceptions (not recommended) or you can take some simple actions to reverse them. One easy way for **inspiring** Millennials (without having to inappropriately promote them) is to show your trust in them by offering some schedule flexibility. Show your Millennials you believe in them by not requiring them to be in the office eight a.m. to five p.m. Be clear about the results you expect, and then trust them to work on the project on a schedule that better fits their lives. Trusting your Millennial employees with a flexible schedule will reinforce their self-esteem and motivate them to deliver the results you need.

GENERATION Z LEADING GENERATION Z

As you likely already know, Generation Z is the most diverse generation ever. Beyond race and gender, we have employees who migrated from different countries, come from unique family backgrounds, plus different religions and sexual orientations to name a few. More than just the existence of this diversity, Gen Z is also the most accepting of different generations. They love learning from each other and embrace different perspectives. When **recruiting**

Gen Z, promote your desire to have a diverse employee population. This will resonate with people who consider themselves diverse but it also will resonate with white males of your generation who want to be a part of an organization that cares about diversity.

Generation Z is motivated by online contests. This may mean achieving the next level on *Fortnite* or the latest version of *Call of Duty*. If they aren't into fighting others on screen, members of Gen Z are almost certainly motivated by keeping their social media streaks alive. Beyond sharing updates, SnapChat and other social media apps keep track of how many days in a row they've snapchatted a friend. Streaks go on for years, and they become an important part of Gen Z's daily routine. Brian's son even gave his password to a friend so he could continue his streak while on a Caribbean cruise without Internet access (that is, until Brian and his wife found out and stopped the sharing of passwords)! This is why gamification can be such an important part of **training** Gen Z. Your training participants are already wired to look for ways to "win" and by building in gamification to your curriculum, you'll have them logging in to complete tasks to earn their "prize" (and learn something along the way).

You have an advantage others may not in leading members of Generation Z. As a Gen Z yourself, you understand they are tech savvy, and you know you won't have to teach them how to use a tool; they'll figure it out for themselves. With that in mind, leverage technology when **managing** Gen Z to simplify their daily tasks. Ask them to find creative ways to make their lives easier and they'll jump on the opportunity. You can also use technology from a managerial perspective. For instance, salesforce.com (a client relationship management system for sales people) has myriad configurations and can be connected to hundreds of associated apps. Most organizations don't use Salesforce's full capabilities because their sales people get confused trying to navigate the technology. With Gen Z's expertise, they'll be utilizing far more aspects of the system while providing you the data you need to manage them as effectively (and efficiently) as possible.

It's **inspiring** for every generation to work for something more than a paycheck, but no generation feels this more strongly than Generation Z. They saw the effects of the Great Recession on their parents—lost jobs and lost savings—despite working hard. Even at a young age, they realized that there has to be more to working than trying to keep your job. Gen Z wants to work for the greater good of society. They want to change the world. And they want to get paid for doing it. When you can tie Gen Z's work to a greater purpose, you'll keep them motivated to do (and continue doing) awesome things for your organization.

LAGNIAPPE: FOLLOWERSHIP

"The best way to make a movement, if you really care, is to courageously follow and show others how to follow."

– Derek Sivers

This book has been about leadership. How to get the most out of every one of your employees—regardless of their generation. As with all of Stan's books, though, we'd like to give you a little extra. The lagniappe. Not familiar with lagniappe? It's a creole word that means "to give more." It's that little something that's thrown in for good measure. Mark Twain described lagniappe is his autobiography *Life on the Mississippi*, "... a word worth traveling to New Orleans to get."

It doesn't matter what kind of leader you are, what your place is in your organization's hierarchy, or what kind of organization you work for, you all have a common characteristic beside being a leader. You're all followers. Regardless of your leadership role, you follow someone. It might be the manager above you, it might be the CEO of your company, it might be your Board of Directors. You're taking direction from someone.

"Aha!" you say, "I'm an entrepreneur. I don't report to or follow anyone." Yes, you do. Even if you're at the very top of your organization, you answer to someone—your customers.

For that reason, we wanted our lagniappe to address briefly something every leader has to consider—how to be a great follower. As a leader, you know how much easier life can be when an employee meets you "half way." When the responsibility for creating a great team doesn't rest solely on the shoulders of the leader, a team's performance accelerates. You know this to be true in your leadership role, and this section of the book is to help you become your leader's favorite employee. Imagine if you understood why your manager made the decisions he/she did. Imagine if you could match the style of your leader(s) (if only for moments at a time) to be more successful. Who do you think your leader is going to ask to work on the best, highest-visibility assignments that earn people more money and promotions? The employee who constantly chafes at the leader's style and approach or the one who seems to align with it at all the critical moments? We're not talking about being a butt-kisser here. We're talking about you helping your manager be the best leader he/she can be by you understanding their generation.

CASE IN POINT: Theo Epstein, president of baseball operations for the Chicago Cubs, became the youngest GM and one of the most important people in Major League Baseball through followership. Epstein believes in what he calls the 20 percent rule. Theo explained this to David Axelrod on The Axe Files, "Whoever your boss is, or your bosses are, they have 20 percent of their job that they just don't like ... so if you can ask them or figure out what that 20 percent is, and figure out a way to do it for them, you'll make them really happy, improve their quality of life, and their work experience."[123]

Let's take a brief look at what it takes to be an awesome follower for each generation.

FOLLOWING MATURE LEADERS

You've got it now. You know Matures are tough. They became frugal greatly influenced by the Great Depression, persevered in very tough times, and almost always put service before self. If you're working for a Mature, these are the characteristics for you to highlight.

Mature Follower Tip #1: Be conservative with your budget

The company is growing revenue, you're turning a profit, and it feels like it's time to slow down your busy schedule a little by hiring some extra people. Maybe. If you're not from the Mature generation, though, you're probably thinking of spending more money than your leader has in mind. Before you ask your Mature leader for

---

123. https://www.cnbc.com/2017/01/19/theo-epstein-of-the-cubs-shares-his-20-percent-rule-for-getting-ahead.html

extra budget to expand your team, ask yourself if you can do more with what you have. Can you get more efficient? Can you get a little more out of your subpar employees? Can you swirl a little water in that jar to get the last bit of jelly before buying a new jar? If you've done all of these things, then go to your Mature leader to ask for more funding. And have proof of how you've maximized resources and your team really is running on all cylinders before you make the ask.

Mature Follower Tip #2: Stay upbeat in tough times

Said another way, don't whine. Matures (or their parents) survived the Great Depression and World War II. They're from a generation who watched 25 percent of their coworkers die on bombing missions on a daily basis and still they kept coming to work. How's it going to sound when you complain about your morning commute or that your office is too cold? Your Mature leader is going to be thinking, "Suck it up!" and start looking for another employee that exudes the fortitude they hold dear. Matures know when times are tough, and they'll appreciate it when you work through those hard times without complaining.

Mature Follower Tip #3: Service before self

Matures were raised to help each other and their communities. When five percent of the nation is homeless and 50 percent of children don't have enough to eat, communities pull together. You likely won't experience anything close to those hardships, but you will have the opportunity to look out for others. In your Mature leader's eyes, there's nothing more important than taking care of those that need extra help. To that end, make sure your team has everything they need (both equipment and training) to be successful. See where you can help a peer accomplish something they struggle with. Your Mature leader will be looking for this and when you show your consistent desire to look out for others, you'll put the spotlight on yourself as someone who should be groomed for upper management.

FOLLOWING BABY BOOMER LEADERS

Baby Boomers take great pride in their work. They consider their position a status symbol and are largely defined by their employment. In their mind, it took a lot of blood, sweat, and tears to get to where they are today, and they respect the same sort of dedication from their employees. By aligning with their ideals, you'll shine in their eyes.

Baby Boomer Follower Tip #1: Live with and be prepared to provide detail

Baby Boomers care about detail. They want to share detail (some would say excruciating detail) with you when they're teaching you something new, and they expect you to provide them detail in return. Live with it. When your manager is giving you a blow-by-blow description of how things used to be at your organization and how they've changed, listen. Ask questions. Appear to care. It may seem meaningless, but it will go a long way. When briefing your leader on your project's status, be prepared to offer detail. Sometimes executives just want a quick overview, so you don't need to necessarily start with all the detail, but be ready to "peel the onion" when asked. Many Baby Boomers want to understand all the steps you're taking to accomplish your goal and you'll want to be ready to provide them.

Baby Boomer Follower Tip #2: Be a lifetime learner and enable them to be one as well

It doesn't matter that Baby Boomers are nearing the end of their careers; they love to learn. Unlike previous generations, they want to continue to learn new techniques and new technology even into retirement. As their employee, you'll connect with your Boomer leader by taking an active role in your own continuing education. Send your manager articles about work topics you found interesting and, more importantly, ask them about their own experiences. Your desire to learn from your Baby Boomer leader will make you a kindred spirit viewed in a positive light. And, you'll learn how to do your job better.

Baby Boomer Follower Tip #3: Show your work (and how hard you're working at it)

Remember how your elementary school teacher always wanted you to "show your work" on math problems? "But I got the right answer!" you'd complain, and the teacher still took off points. They wanted to ensure you learned the techniques and didn't create some kind of short cut to find the answer. The same goes when you work for a Baby Boomer. They want positive results, but they also want to see you working to get those results. "If I can't see you working, you're probably not," is a common thought among Boomers. This is going to be tough for Millennials and Gen Z, but to excel working for a Baby Boomer, you need to show how hard you're working. This may mean coming in early or staying late even though you could easily accomplish the same tasks with your laptop at home. By being physically present and working hard, your Boomer leader will feel more comfortable you aren't skipping any steps to get to the right answer.

FOLLOWING GENERATION X LEADERS

Despite being recognized enough to be placed in a leadership position, Generation X still doesn't trust upper management. Because they were often left alone to create their own path, they are self-oriented (not to be confused with selfish) and are looking to get their work done, get credit for that work, and still have a little fun along the way.

Generation X Follower Tip #1: Keep it brief

Nothing grates on a member of Generation X like wasting time. Worthless meetings, needless conversations, and unnecessary detail go over like a lead balloon to Gen X. When providing a project update to your Gen X leader, hit the highpoints and be ready to move on. Of course, you'll need to have detail in your back pocket in case there are questions, but don't tell your story hoping for the big "reveal" at the end. Begin with the bottom line upfront and then highlight key details. You'll end up with more frequent and higher quality time with your Gen X leader if they know every meeting isn't going to take an hour.

Generation X Follower Tip #2: Recognize credit where credit is due

It may sound funny, but everyone likes to get credit for their hard work—even leaders. This is even more true for members of Generation X. As they aren't the most trusting souls to begin with, if they see you trying to steal credit for their work, you'll be on their naughty list. Celebrate your accomplishments and celebrate theirs. Once your Gen X leaders see you're looking out for them, they'll lean toward making sure you get more credit than you may deserve. Just make sure that's their choice and not yours.

Generation X Follower Tip #3: Make work fun

Generation X was the first generation to look for fun in their daily business lives. Remember the vending machine challenge from earlier in the book? That was a Gen X creation. If you want to be a good follower of Gen X, first do a great job! There's no substitute for exemplary performance. However, if you'd like to stand out, try to make work more fun for your team and your Gen X leader. Be the person who creates the NCAA basketball pool or starts a fantasy football league. Your leader will appreciate the diversion, and you'll get some extra time with your manager to learn how to be a better employee.

FOLLOWING MILLENNIAL LEADERS

As the generation that will soon represent 50 percent of the workforce, Millennials are in a unique situation. They are rapidly taking on leadership roles while still being on the younger end of an organization's employees. This situation brings with it a desire to prove their worth in leadership roles while also bringing a tinge of doubt as Millennials ask themselves, "Am I really ready for this?" Helping your Millennial leader get over that hump and excel will make you a valuable employee.

Millennial Follower Tip #1: Consider suggesting a (reverse) mentoring arrangement

Since many Millennial leaders are landing their first leadership roles, they are a little unsure about their leadership abilities. They want to prove their worth quickly, but they also have enough self-awareness to realize they don't have everything figured out. That's where older generations can step into a mentor role—even if for your direct manager. Offer your perspective in a private, non-threatening way that enables the Millennial to learn from your experience without losing face. Take the stigma away from a subordinate mentoring a leader by asking your Millennial manager for guidance. They'll appreciate both your desire to help them and your desire to follow their lead.

Millennial Follower Tip #2: Embrace multi-tasking

Older generations can struggle with the idea of multi-tasking. They like to do one task at a time until all are complete. Millennials don't think this way, and if you insist on working all your tasks in serial, they'll think of you as an old dog who has trouble learning new tricks. If you're uncomfortable with multi-tasking but still want to follow your Millennial's lead, work on your various tasks in one-hour segments. Focus on one project at a time and then switch to the next. At the end of each day or week, you'll have moved a variety of initiatives forward (like your Millennial manager wants) while still keeping your brain straight.

Millennial Follower Tip #3: Organize group learning or other activities

Millennials were raised to work in groups. Their parents arranged play dates from an early age, and teachers designed many school projects as team activities. As we've shared, that means Millennials can struggle when it comes to managing projects on their own. If you want to be a great follower, organize group learning or other activities. Your Millennial leader will have a better chance to thrive in that environment, and you may pick up some ideas from the other participants. Your leader will appreciate you creating an atmosphere of continual learning that advances your entire team.

FOLLOWING GENERATION Z LEADERS

Just due to their age, if you have a Generation Z leader, it's likely their first "work" leadership role. That means they may be somewhat inconsistent in their leadership approach (as we all were). You'll need to be patient with that and roll with the punches. Like other generations, they'll figure it out, and if they learn leadership with the speed they learn other things, they'll likely understand leadership faster than their forebearers.

Generation Z Follower Tip #1: Be quick and frequent

Generation Z is not used to waiting for results. As the first true digital natives, they've never known a world where they couldn't ask Siri or Alexa for an immediate answer. That means they're going to use technology for all the easy answers, and you'll be left with the harder problems to solve. It also means that the minute you're asked to complete an assignment, you'll be on the mental clock to complete it quickly. Because most projects can't be completed in hours or even days, be sure to provide your Gen Z leader with frequent updates. That way, your leader will know you're making progress even though it takes you longer than Siri to come back with an answer.

Generation Z Follower Tip #2: Work/life integration

Previous generations (especially Gen X and older) think in terms of work/life balance. They are willing to work hard for the organization, but they also want to have their time off (even Baby Boomers). Gen Z, however, thinks in terms of work/life *integration*. They'll work on projects from a café, at home, and while waiting for their meal at a restaurant. As their employee, you need to be prepared to do the same. It's going to feel intrusive to have to check your phone for messages and emails in the evening, but that will be normal for your Gen Z leader. It's okay to set boundaries like, "I'm going on vacation next week and will have spotty cell coverage." Gen Z will respect that—they just won't understand if you are unreachable after five p.m. every evening.

Generation Z Follower Tip #3: Get onboard with tech

Generation Z is very quick to learn new technology. Upon receiving a new tech tool (Apple watch, phone, computer program, etc.), they'll sit down to figure it out immediately—and without instructions. If you intend to keep up with your Gen Z leader, you'll need to get tech savvy yourself. Older generations may want to stick with the processes they know best, but you'll soon find you won't be able to communicate with your manager if you don't stay aligned with their tech. Project management software, group communications, and social media have all advanced significantly in the last few years and show no signs of slowing down. If you insist on using Microsoft Project while everyone else is on Basecamp, you'll quickly drop from the information loop and have a tough time doing your job.

PART IV

FINAL THOUGHTS

FIVE MAIN TAKEAWAYS

We hope you enjoyed the book and that it has made you think—and possibly reassess a few things. Here are five final points for you about Gray Goldfish and leading across the generations:

1. NO ONE-SIZE-FITS-ALL APPROACH TO LEADERSHIP

There isn't always a clear-cut path to great leadership. There is no black and white approach to success. You'll have to use a variety of techniques to overcome challenges and get the most from your employees. A one-size-fits-all approach is a recipe for disaster because your employees approach their work differently. You're going to have to navigate plenty of gray areas to find the approach that works best.

2. GEN Z IS NOW THE 5TH GENERATION IN THE WORKPLACE

Generation Z has reached the workplace. We now have to engage employees across five generations. Engaging today's workplace is vital to business success.

3. NO SECOND CHANCES TO MAKE A FIRST IMPRESSION

It's important to get off on the right foot. Employees make the critical decision to stay or leave within the first few months on the job. Leaders can maximize retention, engagement, and productivity by focusing on a strong first impression.

4. KNOW THY SELF

In order to lead every generation, you need to know how to lead *in the context* of your own generation. That means understanding your own generational tendencies as well as the tendencies of those you follow.

5. FOLLOWING IS AS IMPORTANT AS LEADING

Regardless of your leadership role, you follow someone. It might be the manager above you, it might be the CEO of your company, it might be your Board of Directors. You're taking direction from someone. You need to become your leader's favorite employee. Understand the importance of following and help your manager be the best leader he/she can be by you understanding their generation.

ADDITIONAL INSPIRATION AND FURTHER READING

Decoding Gen Z, Mark Beal

Employees First, Customers Second, Vineet Nayar

Empower. Promote. Launch. [REPEAT], Jeremy Graves

Generations at Work, Ron Zemke, Claire Rainers, and Bob Filipczak

Green Goldfish 2.0, Stan Phelps and Lauren McGhee

Millennials & Management, Lee Caraher

Not Everyone Gets A Trophy, Bruce Tulgan

Sticking Points, Haydn Shaw

Ties to Tattoos, Sherri Elliott

Turn the Ship Around, David Marquet

Unlocking Generational Codes, Anna Liotta

Us vs. Them, Jeff Havens

When Generations Collide, Lynne Lancaster and David Stillman

When Millennials Take Over, Jaime Notter and Maddie Grant

Work With Me, Debra Magnuson and Lora Alexander

Would You Do That to Your Mother?, Jeanne Bliss

You Raised Us, Now Work With Us, Lauren Rikleen

Yellow Goldfish, Stan Phelps and Rosaria Cirillo Louwman

ABOUT THE AUTHORS

STAN PHELPS

Stan Phelps is a best-selling author, keynote speaker, and workshop facilitator. He believes that today's organizations must focus on meaningful differentiation to win the hearts of both employees and customers.

He is the founder of PurpleGoldfish.com. Purple Goldfish is a think tank of customer experience and employee engagement experts that offers keynotes and workshops that drive loyalty and sales. The group helps organizations connect with the hearts and minds of customers and employees.

Prior to PurpleGoldfish.com, Stan had a 20-year career in marketing that included leadership positions at IMG, adidas, PGA Exhibitions, and Synergy. At Synergy, he worked on award-winning experiential programs for top brands such as KFC, Wachovia, NASCAR, Starbucks, and M&M's.

Stan is a TEDx speaker, a Forbes contributor, and an IBM Futurist. His writing is syndicated on top sites such as Customer Think and Business2Community. He has spoken at over 300 events across Australia, Bahrain, Canada, Ecuador, France, Germany, Holland, Israel, Japan, Malaysia, Peru, Russia, Singapore, Spain, Sweden, UK, Vietnam, and the U.S.

He is the author of nine other business books and one fun one:

- *Purple Goldfish - 12 Ways to Win Customers and Influence Word of Mouth*
- *Green Goldfish 2.0 - 15 Keys to Driving Employee Engagement*
- *Golden Goldfish - The Vital Few*
- *Blue Goldfish - Using Technology, Data, and Analytics to Drive Both Profits and Prophets*
- *Purple Goldfish Service Edition - 12 Ways Hotels, Restaurants, and Airlines Win the Right Customers*
- *Red Goldfish - Motivating Sales and Loyalty Through Shared Passion and Purpose*
- *Pink Goldfish - Defy Ordinary, Exploit Imperfection, and Captivate Your Customers*
- *Purple Goldfish Franchise Edition - The Ultimate S.Y.S.T.E.M. for Franchisors and Franchisees*
- *Yellow Goldfish - Nine Ways to Drive Happiness in Business for Growth, Productivity, and Prosperity*
- *Bar Tricks, Bad Jokes, & Even Worse Stories*

Stan received a BS in Marketing and Human Resources from Marist College, a JD/MBA from Villanova University, and a certificate for Achieving Breakthrough Service from Harvard Business School. He is a Certified Net Promoter Associate and has taught as an adjunct professor at NYU, Rutgers University, and Manhattanville College. Stan is also a fellow at Maddock Douglas, an innovation consulting firm in Chicago. Stan lives in Cary, North Carolina, with his wife, Jennifer, and two boys, Thomas and James.

To book Stan for an upcoming keynote, webinar, or workshop go to stanphelpsspeaks.com. You can reach Stan at stan@purplegoldfish.com or call +1.919.360.4702 or follow him on Twitter: @StanPhelpsPG.

BRIAN DOYLE

Brian is a recognized expert in helping organizations lead the five different generations
in today's workforce, speaking and consulting with audiences worldwide. He believes
we don't have enough great leaders in this
world and is working to develop more of
them within every generation.

Brian's leadership experience began as a U.S.
Air Force pilot where he commanded 31 combat missions protecting refugees in Kosovo. Traveling to 40 countries and six conti-
nents, he also transported the U.S. Presidential motorcade around
the world.

Seeking a new challenge, Brian transitioned to civilian leadership
as a Six Sigma Master Black Belt at General Electric Capital where
he led the Quality program for a 170-person business unit. He went
on to become a Sales and Marketing Vice President at Genworth
Financial where he led members of the four older generations to
double Genworth's market share in 18 months. He's since improved
the leadership and customer experiences for his clients resulting in
over $2 billion in new revenue.

Brian earned a BS in Physics from the United States Air Force
Academy and an MS in Engineering Systems Management from St.
Mary's University. He's also a certified Six Sigma Master Black Belt.
He continues his military service as a Colonel in the U.S. Air Force
Reserve and stays active in his community connecting generations
by mentoring high school students to earn a total of $14 million in
college scholarships over the last 17 years.

Brian lives in Raleigh, North Carolina, with his wife, Heidi, and their two sons, Nick and Jackson.

To book Brian for an upcoming keynote, webinar, or workshop go to doyleleadership.com. You can reach Brian at brian@doyleleadership.com or call +1.919.740.7271. You can also connect with him on LinkedIn at www.linkedin.com/in/brianadoyle/ or on Twitter @bnhdoyle.

OTHER COLORS IN THE GOLDFISH SERIES

Purple Goldfish – 12 Ways to Win Customers and Influence Word of Mouth. This book is based on the Purple Goldfish Project, a crowd-sourcing effort that collected more than 1,001 examples of signa-ture-added value. The book draws inspiration from the concept of lagniappe, providing 12 practical strategies for winning the hearts of customers and influencing positive word of mouth.

Green Goldfish 2.0 – 15 Keys to Driving Employee Engagement. Green *Goldfish* is based on the simple premise that "happy engaged em-ployees create happy enthused customers." The books focuses on 15 different ways to drive employee engagement and reinforce a strong corporate culture.

Golden Goldfish – The Vital Few: All Customers and Employees Are Not Created Equal. Golden *Goldfish* examines the importance of your top 20 percent of customers and employees. The book showcases nine ways to drive loyalty and retention with these two critical groups.

Blue Goldfish - Using Technology, Data, and Analytics to Drive Both Profits and Prophets. Blue *Goldfish* examines how to leverage technol-ogy, data, and analytics to do a "little something extra" to improve the experience for the customer. The book is based on a collection of over 300 case studies. It examines the three R's: Relationship, Responsiveness, and Readiness. *Blue Goldfish* also uncovers eight different ways to turn insights into action.

Red Goldfish - Motivating Sales and Loyalty Through Shared Passion and Purpose. Purpose is changing the way we work and how customers choose business partners. It is driving loyalty, and it's on its way to becoming the ultimate differentiator in business. *Red Goldfish* shares cutting edge examples and reveals the eight ways businesses can embrace purpose that drives employee engagement, fuels the bottom line, and makes an impact on the lives of those it serves.

Purple Goldfish Service Edition - 12 Ways Hotels, Restaurants, and Airlines Win the Right Customers. *Purple Goldfish Service Edition* is about differentiation via added value. Marketing to your existing customers via G.L.U.E. (giving little unexpected extras). Packed with over 100 examples, the book focuses on the 12 ways to do the "little extras" to improve the customer experience for restaurants, hotels, and airlines. The end result is increased sales, happier customers, and positive word of mouth.

Pink Goldfish - Defy Ordinary, Exploit Imperfection, and Captivate Your Customers. Companies need to stand out in a crowded marketplace, but true differentiation is increasingly rare. Based on over 200 case studies, *Pink Goldfish* provides an unconventional seven-part framework for achieving competitive separation by embracing flaws instead of fixing them.

Purple Goldfish Franchise Edition - The Ultimate S.Y.S.T.E.M. For Franchisors and Franchisees. Packed with over 100 best-practice examples, *Purple Goldfish Franchise Edition* focuses on the six keys to creating a successful franchise S.Y.S.T.E.M. and a dozen ways to create a signature customer experience.

Yellow Goldfish - Nine Ways to Drive Happiness in Business for Growth, Productivity, and Prosperity. There should only be one success metric in business and that's happiness. A Yellow Goldfish is any time a business does a little extra to contribute to the happiness of its customers, employees, or society. Based on nearly 300 case studies, *Yellow Goldfish* provides a nine-part framework for happiness-driven growth, productivity, and prosperity in business.

Made in USA - Kendallville, IN
13256_9781732665231